HIP HOP

BRING THE NOISE
the stories behind the biggest songs

Neil Kulkarni

THUNDER'S
MOUTH
PRESS

HIP HOP BRING THE NOISE:
THE STORIES BEHIND THE BIGGEST SONGS

Text and design copyright © 2004 by Carlton Books Limited

Published by
Thunder's Mouth Press
An Imprint of Avalon Publishing Group Incorporated
245 West 17th St., 11th Floor
New York, NY 10011

Published in Great Britain by Carlton Books Limited,
20 Mortimer Street, London, W1T 3JW

Library of Congress Cataloging-in-Publication Number: 2004102429

ISBN 1-56025-586-2

9 8 7 6 5 4 3 2 1

The publishers would like to thank the following sources for their kind
permission to reproduce the pictures in this book.

Corbis: 45, 105; /Bozi: 5, 19, 77, 133; /Lynn Goldsmith: 15, 16-17; /John-
Marshall Mantel: 120; /Tim Mosenfelder: 42, 73; /Marko Shark: 78; /S.I.N.:87

David Corio: 55, 56-57 66, 70, 89, 126

Redferns: Glenn A. Baker: 82; /Paul Bergen: 81; /George Chin: 74;
/Amanda Edwards: 134; /Brigitte Engl: 106; /Chi Modu: 11, 49, 60, 97, 102,
132, 141; /Leon Morris: 12; /Michael Ochs Archive: 28, 63, 64-65

Retna Pictures Ltd.: Janette Beckman: 116-117; /Michael Benabib:
20, 26-27; /Jay Blakesberg: 46-47; /Robb D. Cohen: 8; /Zach Cordner: 84;
/David Corio: 22; /Mo Daud: 38-39; /Vincent Dolman: 35; /Sam Mack: 90;
/Eddie Malluk: 32; /Ernie Paniccioli: 36, 110, 129; /James Patrick Cooper: 7;
/John Ricard: 93; /David Tonge: 94; /J. Scott Wynn: 123

Rex Features: 37, 114, 124-125; /Action Press: 50; /Steve Callaghan:
59; /Everett Collection: 101; /Miranda Shen: 98; /Sipa Press/A.Weber: 69

S.I.N.: Piers Allardyce: 139; /Martyn Goodacre: 137, 142-143

Toby Wales: 52

Wireimage.com: Mike Guastella: 41; /Dimitrios Kambouris: 113;
/Johnny Nunez: 25; /John Shearer: 85

Every effort has been made to acknowledge correctly and contact the source
and/or copyright holder of each picture and Carlton Books Limited apologises
for any unintentional errors or omissions, which will be corrected in future
editions of this book.

CONTENTS

INTRODUCTION

First, an admission of failure. The most important hip hop track in the world isn't included here. That's because I don't know what it is. All I know is that it changes every week. All I know is that it engulfs you with an immediacy that goes beyond any hip hop track you've ever heard before. Crucially, if you're being honest to the way hip hop hits you up, the most important hip hop track in the world is the one you're listening to right now, the new shit that's just arrived and is busy detonating your head. The weird, mental freeze that always accompanies someone asking you to "list" music, the way you have to call a halt to something essentially in flux and look back at a static cannon feels especially unnatural when it comes to hip hop, a music whose entire *modus operandi* and rude health depends vitally on its predatory inability to stop moving forward.

That's not to say being a B-boy isn't a thoroughly nostalgic pleasure sometimes: all of us who've allowed rap music to take us over at some point in the last three decades since its birth get giggly fits when we remember what we wore, the bad trainers and dodgy clothes, the terrible movies, the bad rappers we believed in. That's all easy to write off or cop some wounded, bad-taste pride over: what's harder is getting nostalgic about music which still sounds so immediate, still seems to be pushing to the future even though much of it is as old as the hills. The scary thing about writing this book was encountering tracks I'd forgotten, putting them on as loud as I put them on when I first encountered them (i.e. at parent-repelling volume) and feeling not a warm, fuzzy glow but a Proustian rush of excitement – immediate and total recall not just of the details of your memory but total relocation in that teenage head, with those teenage thoughts, with hip hop driving that wedge between you and them (non-B-boys) just as far in as ever. To list the hundred most important hip hop songs of all time means you have to stop time. But every time the needle drops on a great hip hop twelve, you're propelled into the future.

Of course, that's one of the criteria for inclusion here. hip hop tracks that changed the world, sent rap from ghetto to suburbia, tracks that changed hip hop's development, are the lifeblood of rap. But tracks that spin rap culture into new shapes aren't the only tracks featured here. Some of these tracks were barely noticed on release, but they're included here because classic, underground rap can embody the suggestive reach of the genre, the way a great hip hop record can spin you out in myriad different directions both musically and poetically. So "importance" in a purely historical sense isn't the only reason for inclusion here; simply being great and honest within an already established hip hop lineage gets you in as well.

Some of the listed tracks were quantum leaps, some simply glorious dead-ends. All are included because this is a hip hop book unlike any other, less concerned with the overt and oft-repeated history of hip hop than the psychological legacy these records imprinted on a whole generation. Because hip hop is a way of life, not just a lifestyle accessory: it revolutionizes the way you think about all music, all culture, all of human life. It tears down the very rules of lineage and direct influence that a book like this thrives on. Hip hop resists its own transformation into history because hip hop fundamentally says there is no time but now, there is no originality beyond what we can create from what we have. Hip hop's ability to pull from any moment in musical history and any concept in its combatant's psychological background renders any attempt to codify it strictly, any urge to wrap up the story and tell it how it was, ultimately futile.

Old hip hop records reach forward as well as back. Sometimes hip hop progresses precisely on pivotal moments and pivotal tunes that seemingly bear no relation to what's gone before. And that's partly what this book is about as well. It's not backing away from responsibility for a critic to admit that what's essential to hip hop is what can't be confined within words, and that's the infinite reach of it – the way once it's touched you, it touches everything else in your life and your attitude towards the entire world. But I'd like to admit there are some other limits to what I can say, possibly affecting the way you read things here.

No point denying it: this is a book written by someone not from the land of hip hop's birth, and that's a vital part of what follows. The distance in being an English B-boy both amplifies hip hop's fantastical pull and makes it even more of an obsessive pursuit. This wasn't music we heard on the radio or saw on television, even on MTV. (For much of the eighties, that went for American hip hop fans as well.) This was music you heard in a club, on the street, in your room; it took you far out to the cosmos, deep into inner space, down to the gutter or out into neighbourhoods and worlds you could understand but had never heard rendered so dramatically, so clearly, so powerfully. And, for so long, it was precisely the fact that you felt like only you were in on this shit that made it so special. That's why the basis for any book written about hip hop by a non-American has to be the head and the heart and the soul. 'Cos that's where the tracks in this book did their wonderful damage. And once we got the disease, we were destined for a life of constant relapse. I hope it never ends. Knowing hip hop, it never will.

45 KING

The 900 Number

(12", TUFF CITY, 1987)

A bona fide breakbeat classic that still gets any dancefloor bursting into a riot of shrimping flesh, and a seminal inspiration (whether subliminally or directly) to every instrumental DJ since. Born Mark James, the 45 King cut his teeth as a "record boy" for Bronx-based rap legends Funky Four (pre-Plus One). Watching the hip hop business in operation, the King got a crucial glimpse of the coveted breakbeat records that were the WMDs of DJ stand-offs. Leaving the Funky Four circle in 1983 and DJing in the New Jersey scene, aged 22, King's first production for MC Marky Fresh started getting mad play from Kiss FM's Kool DJ Red Alert. It took another four years of struggle for 45 before he finally burst on to the scene with the acclaim his work deserved. First off, in '87, he threw down some intriguing shapes for Wild Pitch's Latee on the long-lost "This Cut's Got Flava". Then something seismic occurred when the 45 King received a record from Tuff City's Aaron Fuchs. Mark slowed down the sax solo. Slapped it over a bruisingly funky beat. Threw in a horn line ripped directly from Marva Whitney's JB-produced "Unwind Yourself". Instant hip hop classic.

It's difficult to impart how enmeshed in the metabolism of all B-boys "The 900 Number" really is: only something almost instinctive can explain how it still remains such a galvanizing tune for the hip hop universe. It's responded to still, wherever it's dropped, like a call to arms, a battle cry or trigger-phrase hot-wired into every B-boy's internal circuitry.

Being rewarded instantly with a production deal and a long-term contract, the 45 King went on to produce for Shabazz, Chill Rob G and Queen Latifah, but he found the terms of a contract artistically restricting. After bringing out his own unmissable recordings under *nom de plume* titles like The Lost Breakbeats, Breakapalooza and 45 Kingdom, Mark James was finally propelled back into the rap mainstream when DJ Kool recycled "The 900 Number" in 1996.

Remixes and reissues ensued before the man responsible for more snapped necks and twisted ankles in the late eighties than anyone this side of Torville & Dean finally found himself back at the top of the rap game, producing Jay-Z's chart-topping "Hard Knock Life (Ghetto Anthem)" in '98 and Eminem's "Stan" in 2002. Still the 45 King.

50 CENT

In Da Club

(GET RICH OR DIE TRYIN', INTERSCOPE, 2003)

"You can find me in the club, bottle full of bub'/Look mama I got that X
if you into takin' drugs. . . "

"I get shot in the face and it knocks a tooth out of my mouth and now I
make a little hiss sound when I speak, but this is the voice that has sold
nine million records so I got shot in the face for a reason. My music is
definitely a reflection of the environment where I came from in South
Jamaica, Queens. Before I had music, I was in a real negative state. When
I started out I would provide for myself through any means so I could be
a person who done bad things but some people enjoy doing bad things
and that's a real big point because I don't enjoy doing bad stuff."

And "bad stuff" is pretty much an accurate précis of the life of Curtis Jackson,
aka 50 Cent, until Eminem signed him to a seven-figure contract in 2002. 50 lived
through what most rap stars simply posture about. Raised in a broken home,
his mum died when he was eight – an introduction to life's precarious thread.
His dad quickly abandoned him and his grandmother bought him up. As a
teenager, he followed his mother's inspiration and started hustling – crack
dealing was lucrative but carried with it spells in prison, stabbings and
shootings that have only made the 50 Cent cachet of gangsta schooling even
more potent. Spotted by the late Jam Master Jay in '96 and affiliating himself
with the Trackmasters shortly afterward, 50 Cent put together his debut album,
Power Of The Dollar, in a mad rush to get paid. One huge hit resulted – "How
To Rob", a track that gained attention for its details of how Cent would go
about mugging several big-name rappers. Such bravado backfired when, in

**Curtis Jackson, also known as 50
Cent – the Original Wanksta gets
to grips with himself.**

May 2000, an assassin tried to take Cent's life, curiously just up the road from where Jam Master Jay would be fatally shot two-and-a-half years later. With one bullet in the cheek, one in the hand and seven in the legs, Cent was lucky to survive. Columbia Records, shamefully, offloaded him immediately and terminated his contract. For Jackson, things could only get worse.

"I get shot nine times – people get shot by accident once and die. I get shot, I'm in the hospital and I sign a publishing deal. I get a $250,000 deal but I only get $125,000 at that point, and the company realizes I've been shot nine times so they drop the deal. If you can't see past the situation in front of you, you're gonna stay stuck in that rut. That was my situation in Queens. Whenever I'd ask who had money, it was always the people I met when I was with my mother and they had the life, they had the jewellery and nice cars. They gave me permission to hustle, but I was having hard luck too. I wasn't so good at hustling that I wasn't getting caught. It felt like I had to do something else that I could provide with and still be available for my son. My father and my mom passed young so it's important for me to have a relationship with my son that would be better than that."

In the two years after the shooting, 50 returned to the NYC hip hop underground, forming the G-Unit collective and churning out mix tapes that built his rep in New York – not just for his baiting of arch-rival Ja Rule but for the skills with which Cent addressed both his own life and the failure of an increasingly out of touch, hip hop mainstream to remember its roots on the New York streets. Eminem declared on-air his admiration for Cent, and an industry bidding war was on. Shady got his man, signing 50 to Shady/Aftermath for more than a million dollars, and pulling Cent into the studio to work with him and Dre on what was by then the most highly anticipated hip hop LP of 2003. "Wanksta" got a preview on the *8 Mile* movie soundtrack, before "In Da Club" suddenly exploded into a worldwide, hip hop phenomenon.

For a man who's been shot at so many times, 50 Cent could legitimately wonder how come now that he's made it, the fire still keeps coming? The consensus amongst the cognoscenti (aka the clueless) about Cent is that "In Da Club" is a sad display of his (and, by extension, mainstream US hip hop's) one-dimensionality. Always, the assumption is that whatever artist is under consideration must be representative of the whole scope of hip hop culture – so rappers get condemned for being simplistic, monomaniacal, narrow-

minded. Thing is, hip hop's always thrived on a mix of genuine multi-directional genii and single-minded simpletons, simpletons like Schoolly D or Snoop Dogg who are so seemingly engrossed in a single subject, themselves, that their whole career can be seen as one long, indulgent, public confession, with all the self-pity and self-aggrandizement that that entails. To diss Mr Curtis Jackson for being in that company is to deny the undeniable jolt of testosterone that sometimes is the joy of hip hop. When you want your mind expanded, you go to a roots show. When you want your mind imploding, hardened and buzzing on its own internal circuitry, when you want to be hit up the head with a straight fix of pure, uncut adrenaline in a crispy-candy, PCP coating, then you go to a 50 Cent show.

50 Cent's *Get Rich Or Die Tryin'* was the monolith hip hop album of 2003, second to Outkast's *Speakerboxxx* in creativity but a country mile ahead of the rest of the rap pack in terms of impact. You've heard 50 Cent everywhere in 2003, whether it's from the TV, a passing, blacked-out coupé or booming from any place where teenagers congregate (shops, clubs, even playgrounds). The hits, "In Da Club", "Wanksta", "21 Questions" and "P.I.M.P." were huge, crossover smashes, a triumphant worldwide tour mopped up any stragglers, and now Curtis Jackson from Southside Jamaica, Queens, can safely look forward to 2004 and 2005 as perhaps the most discussed figure in hip hop, nay, music, full stop. It's attention you feel Cent's not entirely comfortable with.

Especially when he gets pulled in by the police, questioning him in regard to the murder of Jam Master Jay, who he counted as a friend, not enemy. None of which you'd think Cent would complain about. No such thing as bad publicity, right? As well as being questioned about the JMJ shooting, Cent's also been tied to the FBI's investigation of Irv Gotti's Murder Inc label and its relationship to former drug kingpin, Ken "Supreme" McGriff, and a shooting incident at the offices of Violator Management. He was even jailed on New Year's Eve 2002 for gun possession.

All of this ensured pan-media interest (Cent was perhaps the only rapper to be on the cover of both *Source* and the *New York Times* in 2003) on a massive scale that built the excitement around *Get Rich. . .* to fever pitch and ensured it was the biggest-selling, hip hop debut album in history. Without "In Da Club" that wouldn't have happened. Without "In Da Club" we wouldn't be where we are right now. For good or ill.

Planet Rock

(PLANET ROCK – THE ALBUM, TOMMY BOY, 1982)

"Music's magic, bump bump bump, get bump with some flash/People rock rock to the Planet Rock, don't stop. . . "

Perhaps not just one of the most influential records in hip hop history but a record that some say gave birth to techno, house, every moment in the ensuing decade where European sensibilities – musical innovation and synthesized urban idealism – came into contact with the harsh, city realities of Reagan's failed America. Natural, of course, that Afrika would change history, because he'd been living it all his life. Afrika Bambaataa Aasim was born in 1960 in New York, a time that was a defining crossroads for black identity in America. The kids who would come out of his generation would be the first creators of hip hop, aware of the struggles that had bought them this far, yet hyper-aware of pop culture and the way it could be used for the purposes of liberation. Bambaataa took his name from a nineteenth-century Zulu chief, translating as Chief Affection, and he was the founding father of New York's Zulu Nation, a word-of-mouth community of mainly black street kids.

Zulu Nation and Bambaataa transformed the New York street gangs of the late seventies into the hip hop crews of the early eighties with a deliberate programme of self-improvement, business organization and education. Hip hop was the major underground movement that accompanied rap's birth and it led to a perceived "duty" of social reparation and education that hip hop musicians have attempted (with varying degrees of honesty and success) to emulate and achieve ever since. Bambaataa himself had served time in a gang, the notorious Black Spades as well as other chapters of the NYC gang scene: from 1977–85, his importance was both musical and social, a unifying figurehead for a welter of positive, cultural, hip hop activity, from breakdance competitions to gigs promoting peace and racial tolerance.

Most people wrongly think "Planet Rock" was Bambaataa's first record. "Zulu Nation Throwdown" which he recorded twice for two different Zulu Nation groups (Cosmic Force and Soul Sonic Force) came first in 1980. Signing to Tommy Boy, he then cut the Gwen Guthrie-rippin' "Jazzy Sensation" in '82 and released it under the name of Afrika Bambaataa & The Jazzy Five. "Planet

Rock" came next and suggested something cataclysmic had happened behind the scenes, a moment when Bambaataa cut himself off from the earthbound, disco and funk samples that rap fixated on and firmly propelled himself into an Afro-futurist, sci-fi soundworld no one could've predicted. "Planet Rock"'s roots lie thousands of miles away from the furious amateurism of the nascent hip hop scene and deep in the calm heart of old Europa.

Kraftwerk, the four-piece, electronic music pioneers from Dusseldorf, had a phenomenal impact on black youth culture in the early eighties: "Planet Rock" itself was constructed entirely synthetically from two Kraftwerk tracks. The main melody comes from "Trans-Europe Express" and the beatbox rhythm from the 1981 track "Numbers". "So stiff they were funky," as Carl Craig put it, Kraftwerk almost single-handedly gave birth to the New York electro movement. Crucial to what makes "Planet Rock" so earth-shaking a moment in pop history is the presence of Arthur Baker and John Robie in programming its beats. It's the crushing together of Bambaataa's universal message,

motherland-yearning, ancient Nubian wordplay and the doom-laden, machine-music of Kraftwerk that makes "Planet Rock" perhaps the most strangely prophetic record of the eighties, anticipating as it does the whole mix and miscegenation of white electronica and black funk that would give the world techno, house, jungle and garage. As ever, hip hop doing what it does best. Fucking it up for everybody.

Afrika and crew were lucky enough to get a discount from Isaac-Hayes-style-Cloaks R Us.

THA ALKAHOLIKS

Only When I'm Drunk

(21 AND OVER, LOUD RECORDS, 1993)

"Yeah, I get drunk and can't nobody whoop me/I'm trippin', must be the brew that I was sippin'. . ."

When hip hop mentions alcohol (which is often), it's usually presented in the most upwardly mobile, aspirational way possible. Teenage rappers like NWA eulogized 40s, the big-assed bottles of malt liquor that mark a young B-boy's liquid initiation into adulthood. Gangsta rappers ever since have talked loud and longingly about Cristal champagne and Hennessey brandy as tokens of a moneyed-up sophistication that unequivocally separates them from the hooch-swilling hooligans they once were. When Tha Alkaholiks emerged from the Loud stable in the early nineties, what was so instantly endearing was the fact that they talked about drinking from a knowledge forged in love, a grown-up's way of discussing a grown-up's thirst for that which makes him childish again.

In tracks like "Make Room", "Likwit" and this glug-glug highlight from debut album *21 And Over*, Alkaholiks were never overly proud of their predilection for the bottle, nor did they let it dominate what they had to say: when they did talk about drinking, it was realistic, hilarious and curiously moving. A million miles away from the party gossip and youthful boasting that normally characterized hip hop's relation to alcohol, Alkaholiks talked about the kind of steady, heavy, day-to-day booziness that we could all readily identify with and understand.

Propelled by the three-pronged vocal attack of J-Ro, Tash and DJ E-Swift, Alkaholiks came blasting from the unlikely environs of Ohio. J-Ro, an LA native, had quit school and jobs to practise his craft, making tapes in his bedroom from the age of 13.

Forming a trio with Swift and Tash to play house parties, they swam into the already well-oiled universe of party-down legend King Tee, who was at the time looking for a backing crew. Helping him with *Tha Triflin' Album* and subsequent single, "I Got It Bad Y'All", Tha Alkaholiks were christened by Tee and following support slots with Ice Cube and KRS-One, signed to Loud. *21 And Over* and *Coast II Coast* are perhaps the most luridly, accurately detailed slacker-hop albums ever created and "Only When I'm Drunk" is as low-down and close-up as they ever got. Hic.

Eggman

(PAUL'S BOUTIQUE, CAPITOL, 1989)

"Sometimes hard-boiled, sometimes runny/It comes from a chicken not a bunny, dummy. . . "

Official history, of course, would have "Fight For Your Right (To Party)". Or maybe "No Sleep Till Brooklyn", or "Paul Revere", or any of the tracks from *Licensed To III* that announced the Beastie Boys' explosion on to the world stage in 1986. As ever, official history is for curators and exhibits: of way more living and lasting influence on so many more people is *Paul's Boutique*, still the Beasties' finest album and still the benchmark for psychedelic hip hop ever since.

In a sense, you can read the first chapter of Beasties history as them waiting for the world to catch up, waiting for a slow-moving popular culture to realize that freaks like these moved in their midst. Formed in New York University in the late seventies/early eighties, Beastie Boys were originally a hardcore punk act, playing the same venues and music as heroes Bad Brains and Minor Threat. Adam "MCA" Yauch, Mike "D" Diamond and Adam "Ad-Rock" Horowitz originally convened to play MCA's 15th birthday party. Crucially, Beastie Boys weren't spawned by the inner city streets, but from a primarily white, middle-class and privileged background that kept them out of hip hop for the early part of the eighties, both socially and culturally. It was only on the "Cooky Puss" EP of 1983 that they could begin exploring the underground rap that was clearly firing their imagination. (The EP, later sampled for a British Airways commercial, would eventually land the Beasties forty grand in royalties.)

Signed by friend and fellow noisenik Rick Rubin to the fledgling Def Jam label, Beastie Boys proceeded to piss off the entire planet. *Licensed To III*, their debut album, was only half the story, but a ludicrously entertaining half it was, combining a hooligan, gonzo attitude to music that lionized Schoolly D as much as Led Zeppelin with an equal, let's-piss-off-the-parents glee in the lyrics, which owed as much to Slick Rick as Black Flag. it became album of choice worldwide for everyone who wanted to turn something up loud, close the bedroom door and extend an aural flipped finger to the world – teenage music at its most accurately infuriating and righteous and plain wrong in the head. The chaos that ensued (the caged lap dancers they took on the road, the VW badge-stealing pandemic, the questions in Parliament and the accusations of terminally-ill child-baiting) was publicly useful yet privately ruinous to the internal mindset of the Beasties. Isolated on their label and in the music scene, they were also treated with suspicion by a hip hop culture massively resistant to white kids misappropriating an essentially positivist-minded black movement.

Friction between the band and Def Jam, the former accusing the latter of withholding royalties and the company counter-accusing the group of withholding a follow-up album, conspired to foster a paranoia and doubt in the Beasties camp that kept them from reassembling until 1989 – by which time NWA and Public Enemy had stolen the rap spotlight. The lukewarm reception for comeback single "Hey Ladies" suggested that maybe the Beasties' moment had passed; the album that followed, *Paul's Boutique*, did little better. So why pick a track that wasn't even a single from an oft-forgotten album to represent the Beasties' importance in this book?

Because *Paul's Boutique* is one of the greatest hip hop albums ever made, a psychotropic investigation of the damage done but with the needle still

jacked up the arm, pumping the mind full of endless regressions. Every coherent thought that occurs on *Paul's Boutique* cries out for relief from the mental chaos surrounding it but always ends up being pulled into a wildly flailing slipstream that takes in everything from the Old Testament to *Taxi Driver* to seventies kids' television to fifties B-movies to infinity. So the occasional moments of real lucidity take on the same maximal value/minimal importance as everything else: the narrative of the album emerges like the effluent from hallucinating brains, unsure if the images flickering before them in their ratty-assed NYC-drugged-out reality (it's a stoner's delight, *Paul's Boutique*, the kind of diseased logic that seeps from the lips of someone who's stayed in for a year) are as potent and real as the visions all that acid and meth and PCP is giving them.

Musically, it set a new high-watermark in terms of sonic invention, in terms of the sheer breadth of the Beasties' stylistic palette – tracks veered from souped-up, seventies funk to phased-out, Sabbath-metal to hyped-up, Friday-night, partay-down disco to bong-fugged dub, with the Beasties' fragile hold on themselves gradually slipping into darkness and decay. "Eggman" occurs at some point on side one; it doesn't matter where. What matters is that in its mix of Curtis Mayfield loops, Son-Of-Sam-style, paranoiac revenge-fantasy and cartoon lunacy, it perfectly encapsulates everything that's great about *Paul's Boutique* – a document of the wreckage growing up and old and out of it in America can do, but a document that refuses distance and prefers to plunge you right into that queasy, strung-out state the Beasties had found themselves washed up in. *Paul's Boutique* was perhaps the first and finest bedroom hip hop album, a record to get engrossed in privately and completely, precisely because the rest of the world was looking the other way. The man in the street didn't have a fucking clue that hip hop was tearing up the paving slabs he was walking on and making the whole world bend out of shape.

Alongside Happy Mondays' "Twenty Four Hour Party People", it's an absolutely crucial snapshot of a mindset out of control and on the precipice between death and deliverance. The Beasties found a way out. A lot of us couldn't and didn't want to find a way out of the myriad derailments and digressions of *Paul's Boutique*. We lived in our headphones for the next decade. And that, beyond VW badges and bad tracksuits, is the real harm the Beasties did to the world. They made a generation run away from home. Then they helped us go slowly insane in one-bedroom apartments and bedsits worldwide. All hail.

No Beetle is safe. The look that pissed off hatchback car owners around the world.

THE BEATNUTS

Psycho Dwarf

("INTOXICATED DEMONS" EP, RELATIVITY, 1993)

"I wanna fuck, drink beer, and smoke some shit."

A true classic from the mid-nineties' golden age of underground, under-appreciated hip hop from New York. The Beatnuts' debut EP, "Intoxicated Demons", was one of those records you discovered by word of mouth, one of those records you then felt duty bound to press into the lives of everyone you could. What a stunning suite of musical genius it still is, perhaps the most inventive use of obscurantist loops and filthy, irresistible beats this side of Premo's productions. Lyrically, somewhere between idiot-savant and plain idiot-idiot, always framed by some incredibly complex yet utterly immediate beats.

The Beatnuts have been doing much the same ever since, but nothing carries the same charge or has ever made the impact of this introduction to their warped, wonderful, lurid, lucid universe. Blunts (rapper Fashion actually delayed the release of "Intoxicated Demons" by getting imprisoned for six months on a drugs charge), drinks, women trouble and stupidity – always a little too close to home for comfort. Perhaps because home is what they drew from: The Beatnuts were unique at the time for the notion of sampling themselves and their kids and their neighbourhood rather than stealing dialogue and sounds from obvious, old funk records and movies. It gives everything they do a clammy, verité realness that hits up the alien strangeness of their music in wondrous juxtaposition.

The 'Nuts, based in Corona-Queens, made their name with production and remix duties throughout the early nineties for artists as diverse and divergent as Pete Nice, Naughty By Nature, Da Lench Mob, Cypress Hill, Da Youngster, Chi Ali and Fat Joe. A trio comprising Psycho Les (scary Beatnut), JuJu (posh Beatnut) and Fashion (scary Beatnut again), they'd developed their sound during their time at the mixing desk but really came into their own with "Intoxicated Demons", particularly "Psycho Dwarf" – perhaps their most hardcore moment and a natty contrast to the smooth-like-butter jazz of something like "No Equal".

Underground hip hop, particularly on the east coast but pretty much worldwide, tried for the best part of the following five years to emulate exactly the abstract-yet-hardcore tricks The Beatnuts had perfected in '93. And in a myopic, hip hop attitude to design and iconography (which usually led to album sleeves covered in bad gold chains, worse haircuts and everything else that should be on a porn video), the sleeve of the EP was crucial, hijacking Hank Mobley's original, Blue Note cover art to knowing yet monstrously arrogant effect. The Beatnuts remain underground heroes, although every single B-boy loves them. A paradox you feel they're happy with.

Raw

(LONG LIVE THE KANE, COLD CHILLIN', 1988)

"So if we battle on the microphone, bring your own casket and tombstone/And I'm a preach your funeral. . . "

It's the look. And the voice. And the fact that even as you remember him, recall the toe-curling embarrassment of that track with Rudy Ray Moore, the enlightened sexual politic of "Pimpin' Ain't Easy", look at the daffy shit he's wearing on the sleeve of the mind-boggling *Taste Of Chocolate*, recall those faintly unsavoury pictures in Madonna's *Sex* – even at that moment, and it's a moment that comes to everyone who's ever dug the Daddy, when you reckon you just might guffaw your gooch off, you're still pulled in by those "come-to-my-crib" eyes and those "I-might-just-chop-you-up-and- dump-you-in-the-woods" eyebrows. Big Daddy Kane is funny as fuck. But I still wouldn't say that in front of him. Camp he might be (and that's why we love him), but like he says himself, "There's no hair on my chest, but I'm one tough cookie. . . who said you have to be 100 per cent masculine in order to be in?" That's a hip hop god, right there.

Weird that the self-styled "black, gentleman vampire" got his first leg-up (as opposed to leg-over) from self-styled "black, adolescent numbskull" Biz Markie: Markie helped Kane meet Marley Marl and Roxanne Shante who'd work for and be worked on by Kane respectively. Cold Chillin' signed BDK in 1987 and "Raw" was his first single, showcasing Kane's uniquely fast flow and lightning-speed rhyming, always perfectly complimented by his DJ, Mr Cee's deeply funky grooves. The album that followed, *Long Live The Kane*, is still a classic of eighties hip hop (although the tell-tale signals of BDK's lothario/lech persona are already there) and "Raw (Remix)" (alongside "Ain't No Half Steppin'") is its highlight, a furiously paced, totally blazing party stomper that manages to get any room sweaty as hell just so we can watch BDK glide out the door, cool as ice, toting a woman on each arm.

Kane's imperial persona and raw rhyming was a colossal influence on the styles of rappers like Biggie (Smalls) and Jay-Z. Through all his lover-man moves, stylish wardrobe (dig those shoulder pads) and sophisticated, medallion-man charm he really was a blindingly good rapper and an original member of the Juice Crew (also featuring Marley Marl, Roxanne, Biz, Kool G Rap, MC Shan and Master Ace), honing his technique through innumerable freestyle battles. And the props and help he gave back to hip hop, to Kool G Rap, to Biz Markie, even to Public Enemy on "Burn Hollywood Burn", was invaluable. A star forever.

BIZ MARKIE

Nobody Beats The Biz

(GOIN' OFF, COLD CHILLIN', 1988)

"I'm guaranteed to rock, I make the ladies scream and shout/I'm bound to wreck your body and say turn the party out. . . "

Don't take your eyes off the clown. He's got shit up his sleeve. Just as you're busting a gut over his antics, he'll change the entire course of hip hop. Harlem-born Marcel Hall was the most playful member of the Juice Crew and seemed to be the MC who chimed the most with the real concerns of hip hop fans in the mid-to-late eighties: bogey-picking, eating jelly, halitosis, the fact that women found him repellent. In a hip hop world that prized coolness and strength above all, he was a mirror held up to us that revealed our true weaknesses while being so pant-shittingly funny he almost created an alternative kind of heroism about those same failings.

Biz started rapping at Manhattan nightclubs like the Funhouse and the Roxy, meeting producer Marley Marl in 1985 and working as a human beatbox (a skill in which he's rarely been bettered) for Marl-connected acts MC Shan and Roxanne Shante. His first set of demos got him hooked up with Cold Chillin' (who'd also signed Biz discovery Big Daddy Kane), and they released his classic debut album, *Goin' Off*. With precious little support from the industry, the album became a word-of-mouth hit based on the underground hit singles "Vapors", "Pickin' Boogers" and "Make the Music With Your Mouth, Biz" – all of which showed that only a fraction of Biz's real talent was finding its way on to tape. What's clear on the majestically moronic "Nobody Beats The Biz" is that his fondness for toilet humour and goofy, tuneless, half-sung choruses almost camouflaged his true talents as a freestyler. His sample-heavy production was, seemingly, a way for someone chronically shy to hide himself in his music.

It's obvious throughout this party essential that Biz gave hip hop a gleefully self-deprecating and totally melodic sense of fun that was lacking elsewhere in rap as everything got atonal and serious. A year later, he broke into the mainstream when "Just a Friend" (a hysterical tale of puppy love gone awry) reached the pop Top 10, and its accompanying album, *The Biz Never Sleeps*, went gold. This flash-in-the-pan success inevitably became a long-term curse. Although often dismissed as a novelty act, Biz was now getting sufficient attention for the British middle-of-the-road popster Gilbert O'Sullivan to sue him over the unauthorized sample of "Alone Again (Naturally)" on his 1991 album, *I Need a Haircut*. Judge Kevin Thomas Duff (for a lot of old-skool hip hop fans, somebody akin to the Antichrist) awarded punitive damages, ruling that "sampling is theft under criminal law".

The sleepless nights and worries this kicked off in the hip hop community would force rap to change direction musically, and in a sense, it created the nineties' new-found sense of minimalism and invention. He released his last album of the decade, *All Samples Cleared!* in 1993, though the patronage of the Beastie Boys and a new generation of old-skool fanatics ensured that he saw out the decade knowing he'd always have a toehold in the rap game. And rap's the only thing strong enough to keep hold of Biz Markie by the toe. Watch the clown.

How Many MCs

(ENTA DA STAGE, WRECK, 1993)

"The mind tricks the body, body thinks the mind is crazy/But when I get the slazy, keep my flow I'm swayze. . ."

Absolute diamond from rap's second classic era, the mid-nineties. What was happening then in hip hop curiously mirrored what had been happening in rock'n'roll in the early nineties: where grunge was the perfect antidote to LA hair-rock, an introverted and downered alternative to a medium whose extroverted energy was starting to feel inadequate and inaccurate to its audience, so B-boys in the mid-nineties were finding that the moneyed-up exuberance and faux-sophistication of gangster-rap was no longer something they aspired to. They wanted music that reflected their own lives, and those lives were, in the main, fairly miserable, fairly dark, fairly fucked up. The focus of hip hop moved, shifted, from the clubs and jolly good company to the basements and bedrooms and headphones and the bleak company of your own rapidly deteriorating sanity.

Enta Da Stage can be seen as the album that charted that inward shift first, leading to a welter of doomy, psychedelic, incredible hip hop (Show & AG, Real Live, Camp Lo, Mobb Deep) that defined the mid-nineties and laid the template for the underground explosion that would come at the millennium's end. Black Moon blazed a trail because they realized that self-sufficiency was the only way to maintain control over their output, a bold move at a time when the industry was perfecting its exploitation of rap. Shifting 200,000 units of their white-label debut cut, "Who Got The Props", in 1991 led to an industry bidding war. Black Moon signed to Nervous offshoot Wreck because as MC Buckshot said, "Whenever anyone signs with a major US company, and I'm talking specifically about rappers, they begin to lose control of their careers, their

destiny." In '91, such anti-capitalist talk was a revelation. Setting up their own production and management companies, Da Beatminerz (Evil Dee and Mr Walt) and Duck Down (Buckshot and Big Dru Ha), endeared them to rap's old-skool strugglers. KRS-One himself declared Enta Da Stage as, "the phattest shit I've heard in a long time".

MC's Buckshot and 5 Ft Accelerator come at the verses of "How Many MCs" with total aggression but it's a new kind of aggression, one not so much created by what they say but what they don't say, the unspoken threats they leave out and the sheer menace that simmers in their silences. Where so much gangster rap before came at you with the defensive hostility of someone trying to protect what's theirs, Black Moon sounded like they had nothing to lose but a grim reality of guns, weed and violence. Like Kool G Rap and Schoolly D, Buckshot sounded totally bereft of ambition beyond being a menace to society, a destroyer of passers-by. The suicidal fantasies of Biggie Smalls and Noreaga's gleeful thuggery both have their roots in Enta Da Stage and tracks like "How Many MCs".

Crucial to what made acts like Black Moon so revelatory was the new, gruesome nature of the music. The Beatminerz production crew crafted beats and bass-loops so subterranean they seemed belched up from the pits of hell. Dark, dark music. Layered with subtle jazz inflections but with every detail flickering over an abyss of bass that seemed unfathomable, Da Beatminerz filtered and fucked with bass frequencies like dub alchemists, taking lush, seventies-funk samples and attacking them with lo-fi effects, Evil Dee letting loops ring out longer than ever before (not so much cut'n'paste as cut and hijack), the beats actually stretched to the point of distortion. Setting the stage for acts like Heltah Skeltah, Smif-N-Wessun and the OGCs, Black Moon more lastingly created a sound that still engrosses underground hip hop nigh-on a decade later.

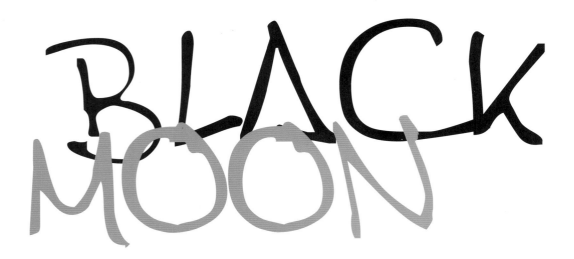

BLACK

The Choice Is Yours

(A WOLF IN SHEEP'S CLOTHING, MERCURY, 1991)

"The styling is creative, Black Sheep of the Native/Can't be violated, or even decapitated. . . "

A glut of riches: Black Sheep were almost too much too soon after the flood of genius that rap collective the Native Tongues had given us. But *A Wolf In Sheep's Clothing* was glorious, undeniable, and this was the single that announced an impending deluge. What was startling about Black Sheep was that here were perhaps the most musically inventive of all the Native Tongues, but rather than pose as furrow-browed, intense explorers of hip hop's cutting edge, they came across as pranksters, comedians, bolshie bastards from the Bronx with a vision they were gonna force on you.

Andre "Dres" Titus and William "Mista Lawnge" McLean met in North Carolina (where they were born) in 1983. One night, Lawnge was sharing a club bill with Sparkie Dee when Dee's DJ Red Alert told him that if he ever made it to the Big Apple, he should give Alert a call. Lawnge did that in 1985, hooking up with the Jungle Brothers and A Tribe Called Quest before phoning Titus to form Black Sheep. There's a hint throughout *A Wolf In Sheep's Clothing* that athough impressed by the Afrocentric consciousness of their peers, the Sheep couldn't help maintaining an out-of-towners' amusement at the po-facedness of their allies. Tracks like "Black With NV (No Vision)" and "To Whom It May Concern" harshly criticized upwardly mobile blacks who turned their back on their roots, while "Butt In The Meantime" and "Strobelite Honey" took a piss-taking attitude toward sexist, hip hop stereotypes that was always pitched precariously between homage and heresy. A textural riot of spoken word, strange accents, knockabout slapstick and splattergun pop reinvention, "The Choice Is Yours" garnered the boys an MTV award for the video and instantly recalls the heady, giddy, pre-sample clearance peak of avant-garde NYC rap. Unmissable.

SHEEP

KURTIS BLOW

The Breaks

(12", MERCURY, 1980)

"Clap your hands, everybody, if you got what it takes/Cos I'm Kurtis Blow and I want you to know that these are the breaks. . . "

There's no point denying it: Kurtis Blow's records don't stand up to the test of time. Play them next to anyone he influenced (and Blow influenced pretty much everybody) and something like "The Breaks" sounds dated, lumbering. There's a tendency with hip hop, as with any musical genre that entails a certain obsessiveness in its fanbase (metal, hardcore) to sepia-tint the past through big-ass, thick, nostalgia-goggles. Thus, everything that happened in hip hop in the early eighties is instantly "classic", the original totemic lynchpins of early hip hop culture become monolithic touchstones – never to be doubted, to the point where if you don't have breakdancers and a DJ and an MC and a graff crew, you're somehow "not hip hop". Ignoring the fact that the whole point of early hip hop was that it was resistant to precisely those ideas of fixed, cultural worth which other, more hierarchical art forms quickly created for themselves, often it simply doesn't sit with the facts to recall those days as some kind of "golden age".

Like the Pistols at the Roxy, in hip hop it seems everyone was in the Bronx and Brooklyn in the early eighties: the fact that most of us had our first experience of rap by virtue of accident, or by virtue of Blondie, seems to have been forgotten. But the modern B-boy has to call it how he sees it – *Wild Style* is a bad movie, Roxanne Shante was a bit of a wild woman, Kurtis Blow was an average rapper. But it's that very timeliness rather than the timelessness of Blow's work which makes it so crucial, such a perfect reflection of a time when hip hop was making it up as it went along, creating and careering over its own boundaries every day.

Before Kurtis Blow, hip hop was happening without the industry's permission or even interest. As the first rap artist to actually shift units, bring in the ackers, Blow is a monumental figure in hip hop history. His popularity and charisma, his success in establishing his personality in the public consciousness as strongly as his music, was vital in proving that hip hop could be more than a fad, more than a purely underground phenomenon.

Commercially, Kurtis paved the way for Flash's Five and Run DMC. He was the first rapper to sign with (and release an album for) a major label, the first rapper to have a single certified gold (1980's landmark "The Breaks"), the first to embark on a national (and international) concert tour, and the first to cement rap's mainstream marketability by signing an endorsement deal. In fact, he was the first really significant solo rapper on record; perhaps the first MC-dominator to lay the groundwork for the Jay-Zs and Eminems of the future.

Born Kurtis Walker in Harlem in 1959, Blow was in on the earliest stages of hip hop culture in the seventies, first as a breakdancer, then as a block-party and club DJ performing under the name Kool DJ Kurt. After enrolling at CCNY in 1976, he also served as programme director for the college radio station. He became an MC in his own right around 1977, and changed his name to Kurtis Blow at the suggestion of his manager, future Def Jam founder and rap mogul Russell Simmons. Blow performed with such legendary DJs as Grandmaster Flash, and for a time his regular DJ was Simmons' teenage brother Joseph – who, after changing his stage name from Son of Kurtis Blow, would go on to become the first half of Run DMC. Over 1977–1978, Blow's club gigs around Harlem and the Bronx made him an underground sensation, and *Billboard* magazine writer Robert Ford approached Simmons about making a record. Blow cut a song co-written by Ford and financier JB Moore called "Christmas Rappin'", and it helped him get a deal with Mercury once The Sugarhill Gang's "Rapper's Delight" had climbed into the R&B Top Five. Blow's second single, "The Breaks", was an out-of-the-box smash, following its predecessor into the Top Five of the R&B chart in 1980 and eventually going gold. It still ranks as one of old-skool rap's greatest and most enduring moments.

BLAHZAY
BLAHZAY

(BLAH BLAH BLAH, MERCURY, 1996)

"You weasel, you better off pumpin' diesel/I find it feasible your days is over frontin' evil. . . "

The best chorus of 1995 went, "When the East is in the house, oh my God!! DANGER!!!" Cutting up Jeru (the Damaja), Q-Tip and the Beastie Boys, Blahzay Blahzay instantly created a rap classic and set out their stalls as New York's new, underground hip hop stars. What set "Danger" apart was the ruffness of the beats (dirty snares, dirty bass, dirty cymbals, all undusted and unblunted from whatever vaults they were dug up from) and the way DJ PF Cuttin's turntable skills actually involved real, itchy, mind-blowing scratching in an era when Dre was busy airbrushing needle-abuse out of the hip hop lexicon.

The Brooklyn duo consisting of DJ/producer PF Cuttin and rapper Outloud first formed their alliance in 1985. Choosing a patient, indirect path rather than the fast track, the duo worked behind the scenes for 10 years producing tracks for artists such as Masta Ace and Craig G. Their big breakthrough came in late 1995 with "Danger", a song that unexpectedly turned into a volcanic crossover hit that tore dancefloors up for months and proudly waved the east coast flag at the time when the coastal beefs were blowing their hardest. *Blah Blah Blah*, the album "Danger" eventually found itself washed up on, was one of the most underrated classics of hip hop's second golden age (check out "Long Winded" and "Don't Let This Rap Shit Fool You'" for definitive, mid-nineties, east-coast hip hop), but "Danger" is in the heart of every B-boy forever.

My Philosophy

(BY ALL MEANS NECESSARY, JIVE, 1988)

"Boogie Down Productions is made up of teachers/The lecture is conducted from the mic into the speaker. . . "

It's the voice. Its commanding power, its quasi-religious tone of declamation and revelation. For someone frequently lauded as a voice of sanity in hip hop, a lone maintainer of conscience and integrity in a business often driven down by mercenary concerns, KRS-One's real power as a rapper often exists in the queasy, unreasonableness of what he says. Not so much in the content (which, always remember, is only a part of the story) but in the style of delivery: Blastmaster KRS-One has one of those instantly identifiable voices in rap that you know you're gonna believe every word from, but you suspect is working some kind of voodoo on you. There's an ole-time Pentecostal fury to his syntax that rains holy terror down on you every time he opens his mouth, making even the most reasonable propositions sound like the apocalyptic, brimstone-tongued declamations of an Old Testament prophet.

It was the dichotomy between the believable and the plain belligerent that made Boogie Down Productions both politically inspirational and hugely pioneering in pure hardcore, a paradoxical testament to KRS's ability to both chronicle and critique the culture he helped create. "My Philosophy", a bass-heavy, ringing statement of intent, is still the definitive BDP cut because not only does it contain a homage to Scott La Rock's murderously minimal way with a beat and loop but it also finds Kris Parker – KRS – at his righteously wrathful best. The barely-there backdrop perfectly showcases his steel-mesh-shattering boom of a voice, while you can already detect traces of the ragga and dancehall touches that would uniquely (at the time) hallmark his work. (KRS's dad was Trinidad-born but deported soon after the birth of his son.)

Bronx based and bred, BDP comprised Scott Sterling and Lawrence "Kris" Parker. Some accounts say that Parker was given the name Krishna (source of the abbreviated KRS) when he was born, while many others state that it was a teenage nickname bestowed upon him because of his spiritual obsessions. He

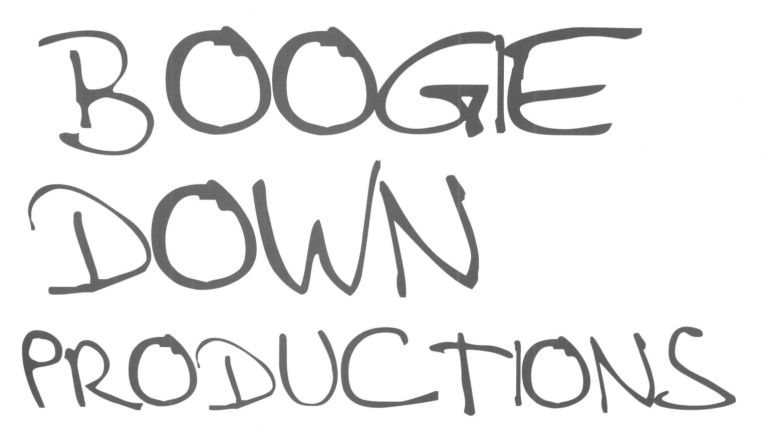

met Sterling at a homeless shelter in the Bronx, where Scott worked as a counsellor and KRS was a client.

KRS had dropped out of school in his early teens, surviving in shelters like this and on the streets while he continued his education, as his own teacher, in the Bronx's many public libraries. At 19, he spent time in jail for selling weed and, on his release, the first social worker to speak with him was Scott. Early BDP (as heard on seminal cuts like "Crack Attack", "9mm Goes Bang" and "South Bronx") created some of the first rap tracks to accurately reflect street life, and street-level success soon came. The debut album, *Criminal Minded*, remains a seminal slab of Nuyorican, hardcore hip hop, produced with the help of Ultramagnetic MCs. After signing to Jive, and soon after the murder of Scott La Rock, KRS followed a more determinedly conscious path that was a colossal influence on the Native Tongues stable, while his Malcolm X affectations also, curiously, helped foster the burgeoning gangsta rap movement. The albums that followed (*By All Means Necessary* and *Ghetto Music*) were pivotal releases in the politicization of late-eighties hip hop, but "My Philosophy" contains all the strands of KRS's rags-to-ranter story in five, pulsatingly pulverizing minutes. Still hard as hell and with a working knowledge of the depths as well.

The self-made rhyme-laureate of early hardcore, KRS-One.

End To End Burners

(12", RAWKUS RECORDS, 1996)

"Rock steadily for more than just dough
Dance to the rhythm and rhyme of Co-Flow. . . "

We weren't wrong for having hope when Company Flow first crashed into our lives in 1995. We weren't idealists when we thought that this was the first genuinely new sound we'd heard in rap since Public Enemy first emerged – we weren't so crassly cynical that we cared about who would be digging it, and that innocence should be prized. We were even dumb enough to think that Rawkus could be bold, new avatars of a hip hop revolution. The word "backpackers" didn't even have any currency at the time; the reflexive self-hatred and reverse-racial inferiority complexes that would break out like a rash across the avant-garde hip hop scene hadn't yet gained such an engulfing weight. So just because the underground renaissance that Co-Flow helped to originate turned so rapidly into a story of broken promises, craven elitism and self-destructive smugness doesn't take anything away from the amazement we felt when we first heard Company Flow.

And just because the suburban, middle-class audience that flocked to the underground after CF hit pissed off the hip hop cognoscenti and the snobs shouldn't blind us to the truth – that, for a couple of years, Company Flow were without a doubt the most exciting thing happening in rap music. For a while back there, independence meant just that. What then happened with Rawkus (there have been reports of many disputes between the label and the artists) and the new independent hip hop (independence lost its quality control and simply became a badge of pride for the mediocre, with a needless hostility to the mainstream) doesn't alter the fact that Company Flow gave their all to hip hop, and rap can only move forward by still listening to what they had to say.

Company Flow's sound was like nothing else in rap. Beyond the sonic bedlam that the Bomb Squad had devised, Co-Flow's main beat creators El-P and DJ Mr Len seemed to be engaged in a whole new way of making hip hop annoying again – irritating to musos; avant-garde in the best, most hostile manner. To many, it barely sounded like music. Beats would slip out of kilter and disappear in oceans of dub, and loops seemingly created from the belches and groans of a studio in trauma would become distorted into derailed digressions of demented detail. The wordplay didn't help to sharpen the focus. On the contrary, Bigg Juss and El-Producto seemed determined to deepen the sense of unfathomable confusion and terrifying psychopathic clarity that the music helped augment.

They formed in Queens in 1992. And perhaps it was the restrictive solo deal that'd kept El-P from recording for so long that explained Co-Flow's untrammeled experimentalism. Perhaps it was simply El-P's completed course in sound engineering that made their debut LP, *Funcrusher Plus* (actually a re-release of the earlier, double-vinyl-only *Funcrusher*), such an ugly, new rebirth for hip hop.

And that's what was crucial. In creating hip hop's most wayward music and most brain-janglingly free-flowing lyrics, El-P was actually returning rap to its original tenets of freedom and originality, so comprehensively forgotten in the slick-assed gangster age Co-Flow were stranded in. Though it sounded so mired in its own abstractions it was barely understandable, anyone who heard Funcrusher Plus knew that they were in on nothing less than the reinvigoration of an art form many had thought lost to commerce forever. We knew it would be influential. And we knew it'd probably take a decade for that influence fully to be felt.

"End To End Burners" was Co-Flow's final bow, a storming synthesis of the invention of their debut and the more straight-ahead formulations that the indie hip hop that followed would investigate. As such, it's the perfect way into the work of Company Flow for the uninitiated, because it gives only scant warning of how intractably life-swallowing their music could be. Come on in. The quagmire's lovely.

CYPRESS HILL

Stoned Is The Way Of The Walk

(CYPRESS HILL, RUFFHOUSE, 1991)

"Hits from the bong, make me feel like Cheech/And I'm kickin' it wit' Chong. . . "

Like all the really memorable hip hop moments, this came at you from God knows where and rocked your soul into new shapes. For so long, Cypress Hill's masterly debut LP was only available on import in the UK, a new holy chalice that you only gained access to by knowing it was there, by hearing the unholy promo of "Pigs" that blew your mind, by bugging out on the gorgeous Beatnuts-heavy beats and the addictive, Mexicano/Cubano delivery that sounded like a whole new antechamber of vocal madness opened up and rushing out screaming.

When you finally got the album, what greeted you was the giddy realization that Cypress Hill had a ton of this shit to drop: the stand-out tracks ("How I Could Just Kill A Man", "Hole In The Head", "Tres Equis", "Pigs", "Hand On The Pump", "Real Estate") so numerous, so damn tastily smoked-up and nasty and burnin' hot it was '91's most-played, most listened-to hip hop LP by a country mile. Anyone who says they were listening to something hipper is a goddamn liar. The sound cooked up for *Cypress Hill* by the Italian-descended DJ Lawrence Muggerud (DJ Muggs) was unmistakable and had the contact-high addictiveness of chicken crank. As influenced by Black Sabbath, Led Zeppelin and Love as the seventies funk that formed the rhythmic basis, it was a heat-stricken grimy buzz that seemed to stalk streets off the beaten path, stumbling into neighbourhoods united not by race but by poverty.

The critical consensus around Cypress Hill was that they were using east-coast techniques of rhyme invention and applying them to west-coast living, albeit a limited, stoner's view of LA life. All bullshit, of course. The Hill, in truth, were reconfiguring hip hop syntax around their own Latino roots, letting in new vocabulary and speaking this weird, new, hybrid pidgin-gangsta in voices quite unlike anything else in hip hop. The whiney, delinquent tones of Louis Freeze (B-Real) and Sen Reyes (Sen Dog) were unique in rap at the time cos they gained authority not from their ability to sound commanding but to sound real, realistic, as if you were walking down a barrio street hearing this ultra-violent, lurid backchat popping out of every passing window, every front stoop.

To be fair to Cypress Hill, they weren't unique at the time for extolling the virtues of weed. Redman and Goats, for instance, were not exactly averse to rolling up the Northern Lights as well. But it's true that Cypress made it sound less like a habit and more like another way of life, a different perspective on reality, an altered state of movement and thought and intelligence. By no means explicitly spiritual about drug use, they were certainly hearty advocates of a constantly bonged-out mashed-upness that could lead to paranoia and violence just as easily as it could to peace and beatitude. And for most hip hop fans, it was cool that here, at last, we could hear our own drug use (for weed will always waft and warp wherever musicians or music fans of any genre congregate) finally accepted by rap rather than roundly condemned by it (and just as Tha Alkaholiks were making self-administered, booze-fuelled brain damage OK as well).

"Stoned Is The Way Of The Walk" is three minutes wherein dissonance becomes space-rock becomes jazz becomes the kind of steadily, mind-jangling funk Miles Davis cooked up in his early seventies zenith. There was a use of silence and echo and delicious detail in early Cypress Hill that showed a real awareness of psychedelia and the weird distance drugs put into your world. Stoned immaculate.

DAS EFX

They Want EFX

(DEAD SERIOUS, EAST WEST, 1992)

All-in-one mini Lenny-Kravitz
romper suits were all the rage in
Das EFX's hood.

"Bum stiggedy bum stiggedy bum, hon, I got the old pa-rum-pum-pum-pum. . . "

Every few years, hip hop goes through a crisis of confidence, becomes sure that it has hit a dead end, starts worrying about whether it's losing sight of what on earth it's for. At such moments of doubt, the old skool, whatever happened "back in the day" becomes a holy totem of forgotten lore, a sepia-fogged set of values that needs restoring, to save hip hop from its decadence and return it to itself.

When Das EFX first emerged in '92, they were hailed for their glorious revival of real freestyling; in a gangsta era of over-serious, clearly crafted, lyrical self-aggrandizement, they offered a way more poetic, yet way more self-deprecating return to the jagged rhymes and free-flowing wordplay that characterized rap's birth. Das EFX were unforgettable 'cos in a hip hop world where so many conscious rappers sounded like they were hectoring you, and gangsta rappers sounded like they were trying to impress you, Das EFX came across as total dipshits who'd stumbled across a way of making genius hip hop from their daffyness. It was a flow composed of gibberish, made-up words, playground syllogisms, bent-double syntax and occasional moments of startling lucidity that combined to speak like nothing else in rap.

Drayz (Andre Weston) and Skoob (Willie Hines) were classic rags-to-riches ragamuffins from Brooklyn. As college friends sharing a mutual interest in poetry, they entered a rap contest at a small nightclub in Richmond, Virginia. Luckily for them, Erick Sermon and Parrish Smith of EPMD were in attendance, and although they didn't win the prize, they did secure themselves an instant record contract. "Dead Serious" charted strongly even though Skoob and Drayz weren't legally allowed into most of the clubs that booked them.

Perhaps it was their youth that led to their unique, anti-logical, lyrical bent. You get the feeling listening to "They Want EFX" (and especially their debut self-production, "Freak It") that these were rappers keen to avoid talking about anything of consequence for fear of showing up their lack of experience. The result was music and lyrics that were pure fun, something rarely achieved without the sacrifice of a rapper's authority. In Das EFX's case, we never trusted the whelping whippersnappers to give us the truth anyhow. An instant transportation device to a golden age of rap.

The Magic Number

(3 FEET HIGH AND RISING, TOMMY BOY, 1989)

"Doin' hip hop hustle, no rock and roll/Unless your name's Brewster, cos Brewsters are funky. . . "

It was as if we'd been watching a black and white movie for nigh on a decade and then somebody came in and asked for the remote and revealed it had been in colour all along. It was like that revelatory childhood moment when you went to your posh relatives' house and realized Bagpuss had pink stripes. It was like the instant when Dorothy steps from her farm-shack drabness into a Technicolour Oz and realizes she's not in Kansas any more. For all the sample-richness of what had come before (Public Enemy, LL Cool J, Ultramagnetic MCs), there was always something rather monochrome, deliberately so, about hip hop until De La Soul.

Partly because anything else wouldn't have seemed so harshly documentarian, partly down to a sense of hesitancy that the new technology of sampling had engendered, people held back as if on the verge of infinity, afraid to be dazzled. Nobody had taken sampling as far as it could clearly go; it was a tool, a device that could be utilized but must never get in the way of the inherently monolithic message of the rapper.

For the rest of the pop world, sampling was a gimmick that could put an "oh yeah" in the cheesiest, assembly-line singles, a stutter in bad records about Vietnam. But if hip hop could take on sampling properly, really explore its possibilities, start playing games with the history of music that made all points accessible and equally open to transformation – then hip hop music could stop just being a backdrop for the words and actually start affecting the way those words came out, the effect those words had on you, the relationship of the rapper to his audience and to his own thoughts. It happened in two places in 1989. In the studio of the Bomb Squad. And in the deranged head of Stetsasonic's Prince Paul, busy producing 3 Feet High And Rising, an album by a three-piece called De La Soul.

De La were New Yorkers relocated in Long Island. Kelvin Mercer (Posdnous) and David Jude Joliceur (Trugoy The Dove) had known each other since the early eighties and while attending Amityville High School, had hooked up with Vincent Lamont Mason Jr (Pasemaster Mace). Doing the rounds of various crews before forming De La in 1985, Mase met a local DJ, Prince Paul Houston of Stetsasonic, who began mentoring the teenagers. Paul instantly recognized that here were three individuals with wildly diverse groundings in music (their parents listened variously to jazz, reggae, calypso and R&B), a sonic eclecticism bred into their bones that Paul wanted to foment more

deeply. Securing them a deal with Tommy Boy (Stetsasonic's label) resulted in "Plug Tunin'" becoming an underground smash in '88, bringing De La into contact with the Jungle Brothers.

While De La taught the JBs about looping and samples, they in turn welcomed De La into the Afrocentric Native Tongues stable. From then on, De La were seen as contemporaries of Queen Latifah, Monie Love and A Tribe Called Quest in the Native Tongues posse. Sure, they shared some of the same positive, conscious attitudes as their friends – a peaceful sunny-side-up vibe that gave De La the gruesome soubriquet, Daisy Age Soul. In truth Prince Paul's production for De La separated them completely from their contemporaries, and it's his story rather than De La's that informs "The Magic Number": take a listen to anything from *3 Feet High And Rising* and you can hear Paul destroying the conventions of hip hop with a lunatic glee and a Hanna-Barbera soul.

Where hip hop seemed desperate to gain validity by sampling classic funk and breaks from the seventies, Prince Paul took the sampler messthetic and applied it to the entire history of recorded sound. His breakneck, lightning-speed, psych-pop production on "The Magic Number" takes in fifties R&B, sixties soft-pop, spoken-word detritus, radio babble, comedy records and language-training tapes, only touching on rap's usual vaults of authenticity (seventies funk and soul) when it needs to make the most artificial of sounds, cartoonish moments of hyper-blaxploitation as jarring as they are suddenly gone. It was that high-speed restlessness, the huge hunger of De La's music that marked it out. Ideas that elsewhere would be spun out for entire tracks (or entire albums, or entire careers) would be chewed up and spat out by Paul's relentlessly short attention span, becoming moments that captivated you as completely as they would sharply, heartbreakingly, depart your realm.

It was hip hop finally catching up with the promise it had made on its birth: here was a whole different way not just of making music but listening to music, using music, destroying the old hierarchies of taste and authorial preciousness (no one before De La Soul would have dreamt of sampling Steely Dan or Curiosity Killed The Cat) by making everything up for grabs, everything bendable into new, gorgeous shapes. And if the world destroyed De La's promise (the lamentable tag "hippie rap", the unintentional chiming of De La's baggy look with UK dance music's sartorial mode, The Turtles suing them over the samples on "Transmitting Live From Mars"), resulting in a bitterness about their success that would characterize the rest of their (always engrossing) career, then the sheer, heart-stopping wow of tracks like "The Magic Number" will always endure. A moment when rap, and pop music itself, looked at the clock, realized the second hand wasn't moving, and everything changed forever.

DIGITAL UNDERGROUND

Freaks Of The Industry

(SEX PACKETS, TOMMY BOY, 1989)

"Should you A, take the time to find a condom/B, you walk right over and you pound 'em. . . "

There's a fine line between sexy and sexist and this fetid delight from the depths of DU's unforgettable debut album stomps over it in seven-league boots. Not actually as nasty as the other album highlight, "Gutfest '89", it's a detailed, lurid account of just what an old, dirty bastard Shock-G could be over peerlessly controlled heavy funk. And it's emblematic of everything that made Digital Underground so much fun, so perfect a genuine alternative to the pomposity and po-faced humourlessness of so much hardcore hip hop at the time. With PE blazing politics and NWA blazing firearms, Shock-G blazed up a big stogie, put on his Groucho Marx snozz and duckwalked into immortality like some perved-up, hip hop Jimmy Durante.

Building virtually their entire musical backdrop from P-Funk samples, what was remarkable about Digital Underground was that they took that homage one stage further, creating the same wacked-out stage personas and totally engrossing (and totally apocryphal) background blarney as George Clinton and crew always seemed to spin out in the golden age of Parliament/Funkadelic. So that in the end the truthful details of DU's rise seemed less important (and certainly less entertaining) than the lies they'd tell to explain it, the real personalities involved only slightly less intriguing (Shock himself had spent several years as a criminal before completing his music degree and hooking up with Chopmaster J to form DU) than the bizarre alter egos they'd inhabit. As immortalized on breakthrough single, "The Humpty Dance", Shock's most

outrageous persona, Humpty Hump, was a mind-blowing, imaginative creation, one of the iconic confections of MC-dom. You were fascinated by this absurdly comic, fake-nosed buffoon with chunky NHS specs and a goofy, stuttering voice (no Morrissey gags necessary) – especially when you heard the tale of his birth.

Apparently Humpty Hump sustained nose-threatening injuries in a freak kitchen accident, but was forced to continue his rapping career with the addition of a false hooter, worn to cover up, *Phantom Of The Opera*-style, the grisly carnage that lay underneath. Of course, with his new, improved snout, he still got pussy, still had fun. The generously slapstick nature of all this defused any accusations that the frequently sleazy lyrics could've provoked, while on *Sex Packets*, it was clear that there was even more imaginative clout behind the Digital Underground story. Based on what sounds like a flimsy premise (the creation and exploitation of a drug that creates wet dreams), *Sex Packets* actually emerges as one of the great concept LPs in rap, a simple and attractive idea inflated along lines both realistic and fantastical. And in the depth of their love and knowledge of P-Funk lay the future of west-coast rap: listen to *Sex Packets* now and you can hear backwards echoes of the entire G-Funk movement that would swallow hardcore rap whole in the ensuing years.

Digital Underground followed *Sex Packets* in early 1991 with "This Is an EP", the first time a young rapper called Tupac Shakur was ever heard by most of us. The future was gonna be different, harsher, more divisive, but in the golden days of DU's "Doowutchalike" universe, hip hop was nothing but a good time had by all. The past, the present and the future wrapped up in pure comic genius.

**Digital Underground
doing the bumpkin dance.**

DOUG E FRESH

The Show

(OH MY GOD!, REALITY, 1985)

"The human beatbox or the entertainer/No other title could fit me plainer..."

What's weird writing about hip hop is that for all the verbosity you can throw around your experiences with this music, there will always be something crucial to your memory that you can't really sum up in words because you can't be a kid again. Being a kid has a lot to do with getting into hip hop. The whole wrong-headed, whiteboy, critical consensus that talks about rap albums (always albums, never singles) as "hip hop for grown-ups" or "the hip hop artist it's OK to like" rests on the fundamental supposition that rap music is essentially kids' stuff, ephemeral, a faddy habit that people will either eventually fall out of or plain forget about. Utterly ignorant of the way a lot of us grew up on hip hop, allowed it to nurture us from adolescence to adulthood. But also, like most clichés, it contains a grain of truth.

There was a yelp, or it might have been a gasp, or a giggle, or a guffaw or anything else more suited to *Beano* characters, that emerged from our dropped, childhood jaws at some point in our relationship to rap. A moment when something so cool, so firing of those same receptors that made "The A-Team" the pinnacle of entertainment and Atari an alternate universe, came crashing into your den-building, bike-riding kidsworld and slapped your head upside down. One such moment for a lot of us was the first moment we heard Doug E Fresh's "The Show".

Cool 'cos of the Inspector Gadget sample. Cool 'cos of MC Ricky D (aka Slick Rick) and his downered delivery. Cool 'cos of the lines that were so much fun to blather around the playground. ("Six minutes Doug E Fresh you're on!" was more popular than Joey Deacon and "Blackadder" quotes in the break-time summer of 1985.) But triple-cool and skill and ace and wicked 'cos of

Fresh's dizzying array of human sound effects (so innovative in their day that Fresh now has his own switch on the Oberheim Emulator) – those weird things and tics that he did with his mouth, that qualified him as "the original human beatbox".

For a summer of nuttiness, everyone was popping lips, popping mouths, doing those stupid waves and spins with their arms. 1985 was truly the summer where hip hop made it beyond specialized interest and into the consciousness of the world's youth. Before you knew it, everyone, everywhere, was trying to copy Fresh's technique, and every rapper on the planet seemed intent on proving they could beatbox (with varying, occasionally embarrassing degrees of success). No one this side of Biz Mark or Large Professor could quite achieve Fresh's ability to replicate drum machines and loops at the same time, sound effects (although that guy in *Police Academy* gave him a run for his money) and large samples of hip hop classics.

It was a solitary talent that took the St Vincent-born, Bronx/Harlem-relocated Fresh to the brink of superstardom. Very few heard his first appearance on a single for Spotlight called "Pass The Budda" with Spoony Gee and DJ Spivey. But no one could forget his astonishing performance in the *Beat Street* movie behind the Treacherous Three. "Just Having Fun" and "Original Human Beatbox" built Fresh's rep but "The Show", recorded with his own Get Fresh crew sealed his immortality. Fresh then very nearly became the first-ever rap superstar (and was among the first rappers to take hip hop to Jamaica's Sunsplash Festival), but instead of capitalizing on the success of "The Show", he would end up in court trying to sue Reality Records for non-payment of royalties for the song. He didn't do his chances any favours by refusing to make another decent record (and that dodgy, anti-abortion track on *Oh My God!* wasn't a wise move) but Fresh was still the first human beatbox in the rap world, and still the best of all time.

The Next Episode

(2001, AFTERMATH, 1999)

"Straight off the fuckin' streets of C-P-T/King of the beats you ride to 'em in your Fleet (Fleetwood). . . "

The next time the music press opens its arms to the heavens and tearfully asks where the next Brian Wilson or Joe Meek or Phil Spector is, tell them straight. He's in LA, sitting on top of a huge pile of cash, and he's laughing his lardy arse off. Dre has been one of the most successful producers of hip hop for nigh on a decade now. There are two identifiable strands in his story. The first starts with NWA's epoch-making *Straight Outta Compton*. Dre hates it. Always has done. "To this day I can't stand that record," he said. "I threw that thing together in six weeks so we could have something to sell out of the trunk." The record that launched Dre's career is such a sloppy embarrassment to the pop perfectionist that he spent the subsequent decade apologizing for it, the only way he knew how – by consistently making the most immaculate, American pop music since Michael Jackson's late seventies /early eighties run at godhead.

The second abiding theme in Dre's career can be traced back to his DJing days in the early eighties at LA's Eve After Dark club. Where other DJs in his World Class Wreckin' Cru prided themselves on the obscurantist, underground nature of their playlist, their seamless flex skills, Dre would start playing electro and breakdancing hits and then, mid-track, viciously splice in huge chunks of Martha Reeves And The Vandellas, The Supremes, The Temptations. His love of production-line pop goes beyond the pure lustre of its sound: he loves the ultimate control it affords the producer. Dre more than anyone else can truly lay claim to being a one-man Motown for the twenty-first century. His success, the fact that his protégés (Eminem and Fifty Cent) have relied on him for their stellar rise, isn't enough to impress on its own, but to win that success with no sacrifice of integrity, no price to pay and no compromise to make is rare and remarkable. He hit upon the most luridly exciting sound black pop had made in a decade, and made it work for everyone who came close.

The back room of Eve After Dark was where Dre, together with future NWA members Yella and Lonzo Williams, would record demos, learning the turntable techniques he'd later bring to NWA. You get the sense that Dre was already teaching himself, surrounding himself with like minds, in it to win it. Seven out of the eight albums he produced for Eazy-E's Ruthless Records between 1983–91 went platinum. His best work for NWA (the hugely underrated *Efil4Zaggin* included, with its Bomb Squad meets P-Funk nutzoidness) was the only thing that saved that group from mediocrity. With Suge Knight holding a gun to their manager's head, NWA released Dre in '92 so he could go co-found Death Row but more importantly refine and perfect his own sound. He called it 'G-Funk'. Like P-Funk but slower, slinkier, always at the perfect pace of a heartbeat or a car wheel or a sun-suffocated sigh. *The Chronic* was the album that fundamentally created the west-coast gangsta sound of the early nineties, and made that sound mainstream.

Pulling from P-Funk and Funkadelic, Dre's production on records by Eazy-E, D.O.C. and, particularly, Snoop Doggy Dogg created a new high-watermark in hip hop's scope of sound and professionalism. These were listening experiences light years away from the amateurism and willful chaos that characterized NWA's rise and fall. "Deep Cover" and "Nuthin' But A G Thang" gave warning, but Snoop's Dogg Style album was another huge leap forward,

**Right, the baby-faced Dr Dre.
Overleaf, the billion dollar
baby-faced Dr Dre.**

breaking sales records and taking gangsta rap to the top of the album charts. Dre was, without a doubt, the driving force behind the wheel. "I can take a three-year-old and make a hit record with him," he said, and no one could doubt it for a second.

For the next four years, Dre's sound would dominate west-coast rap and pop (Blackstreet's "No Diggity" remains one of his finest achievements). The intractability of the problems Dre then got engrossed in (long-running beefs with Eazy, Ruthless, TV hostesses and, finally, Death Row) only seemed to make his return as the century faded even more a startling comeback than most could've hoped for. The Death Row dynasty had held strong until the spring of 1996, when Dre grew frustrated with Knight's strong-arm techniques. At the time, Death Row was devoting itself to 2Pac's label debut, *All Eyez on Me* (which featured Dre on the breakthrough hit, "California Love"), and Snoop

was recovering from his draining murder trial. Dre left the label in the summer of 1996 to form Aftermath, declaring gangsta rap dead. While he was subjected to endless taunts from his former Death Row colleagues, their sales had slipped by 1997 and Knight was imprisoned on racketeering charges by the end of the year. Dre's first album for Aftermath, the various-artists collection *Dr Dre Presents. . . The Aftermath*, received considerable media attention, but the record didn't become a hit, despite the presence of his hit single, "Been There Done That". Even though the album wasn't a success, the implosion of Death Row in 1997 went to prove that Dre's instincts were certainly correct at the time.

Both *2001* and its companion, instrumental version followed in 1999 and, by now, with Eminem firmly secured as the most important rapper in the world under Dre's tutelage, it was clear the king was back to take his crown. *2001*

was murderously effective, a brutalizing reprisal of every gangsta cliché in the book but worked around Dre's finest new music since *The Chronic*. "The Next Episode", from its doomy, cinematic beginning through Snoop's lip-smacking rhymes, is just about the most seductively all-conquering moment Dre's ever been responsible for and proof that this man will have something to say about hip hop's future for a good few decades yet.

Nobody Move

(EAZY-DUZ-IT, RUTHLESS/PRIORITY, 1988)

"I'm in a bank, and it's a little bit funny/Takin' all you stupid motherfuckers' money. . . "

"Eric, he was never a rapper. Dre convinced him to rap 'Boyz-N-The-Hood' and then that little voice, that unique voice he got, took it over. That's what started it" – DJ Yella

Never a rapper. A criminal who wanted to make money from rap. A man who attended a fundraising dinner for the Republican Party and had lunch with the LAPD's Stacey Koon, one of the four, white officers charged with the filmed beating of black motorist Rodney King and later, controversially, acquitted. (That acquittal sparked the LA riots of 1992.)

Eazy-E couldn't help offending everyone, but he was still responsible for some awesome – and awesomely nasty – hip hop. Eazy-E was a man who seemed to peak even before he came to the mic, a mic that froze him in a moment of unbridled self-revelation he could never recreate, a derangement that seemed so one-off it almost demanded its own subsequent disappearance into vague recollection and derision. Listening to the voice of Eazy-E, you can tell he was a criminal. He has that forceful, whiney insistence so many criminals have, but make no mistake: the old, pre-*Straight Outta Compton* solo tracks Eazy made on *Eazy-Duz-It* are still tons of fun, even with – in fact, because of – the dated production, the crude unsophistication of the sampling, the cheesy tape stutters. What makes them so startling even now, the shock

barely eroded by familiarity and hip hop's progression (one year in hip hop equals seven years in the rest of pop), is Eazy's voice. It was the first voice in hip hop that could be called weak, pubescent even, and therefore it was petulantly aggressive in a way that was entirely new. Not the loud, declamatory, polemical baritone of a frontman, this is, rather, the snarly back-chat you'd get from the little thug-rat on the periphery of a gang, the one who overcompensated for his physical lack ("Niggaz My Height Don't Fight") with a streak of brattish, unhinged viciousness that was by turns hilarious, profoundly poetic and plain fucking terrifying.

"Nobody Move" is nihilism taken to a paralyzing extreme: gangsta rap growing hair on its balls for the first time. Where Ice-T hi-rolled by in Ferraris, twitching ice-encrusted fingers, Eazy was rapping about good ol' fashioned juvenile delinquency, drinking 'til your breath stinks, totaling cars, resisting arrests, beatings, jail riots, bitches called Suzi with sub-machine Uzis. Even by the time of *Straight Outta Compton*, while Ice Cube was always the man who would "squeeze the trigger 'til bodies are hauled off", Eazy was "drinking 'til I shit my pants, never getting a dance," and "making you sick, you snotty-nosed prick, now your fly girlies all over my dick". Eazy has been the inspiration for a lot of brat-punk rap since, from the Geto Boys to Onyx, maybe even up to the wasted genius of Ol' Dirty Bastard. For that alone, we salute you.

Eazy's infomercials for his patented invisible car-jack failed to reinvigorate his career.

EMINEM

My Name Is

(THE SLIM SHADY LP, INTERSCOPE, 1999)

"Hi kids! Do you like violence?
Wanna see me stick nine inch nails through each one of my eyelids?"

People call him the hip hop Elvis. Like that's a bad thing. I love PE as much as the next man and, yeah, Elvis never really meant shit to me. But to go from that hostility of cultural expropriation to refusing to understand why Elvis was the biggest star in the world is to miss a whole lot of crucial history, to deliberately disengage from a welter of pop experience that's vital if you want to understand the history of pop. And it ignores the fact that Elvis made some fucking great records. Similarly, it's easy to tag Eminem as somebody thieving black culture to make millions but less easy to admit why he's such a potent voice for white kids who find no similar identification elsewhere in rap. Certainly, it's easy to explain why "My Name Is" remains such a compulsive blast. Because it rocks, dilsnick. Duh.

A protégé of Dr. Dre, rapper Eminem's success became the biggest crossover sensation the genre had seen since Dre's solo debut seven years earlier. Born Marshall Mathers in St Joseph, Missouri (near Kansas City), Em spent the better part of his impoverished childhood shuttling back and forth between his hometown and the city of Detroit. At age 14, he was performing raps in the basement of his high school friend's home. The two went under the names Manix and M&M (soon changed to Eminem), which Mathers took from his own initials.

When Em's mom brought him
to the Jerry Springer show he
certainly came prepared.

Though he started building his rep doing battle rhymes in hip hop clubs (an undoubtedly intimidating way to learn your craft), his uncle's suicide prompted a brief retreat from the world of rap. Mathers returned to find himself courted by several other rappers wanting to start groups. He first joined the New Jacks, and then moved on to Soul Intent, who released Eminem's first recorded single in 1995. Proof performed the B-side on the single and asked Em to start yet another group, D12, a six-member crew that supported one another as solo artists more than they collaborated. The birth of Eminem's first child put his career on hold again as he started working in order to care for his family. The bitterness with which his personal life would infect his music had started. As a mouthpiece for this new-found bile, Em created Slim Shady, an alter ego unafraid to speak the recesses of his sick mind. And life kept feeding that bile. His mother was accused of mentally and physically abusing his younger brother, his childhood girlfriend left him and barred him from visiting their child and he was forced to move back in with his mother, an experience that fuelled his hatred for her and increased his sympathy for his brother.

Drugs and booze helped complete the redneck tragedy and an unsuccessful suicide attempt finally spurred him on to transform his so-far predictable saga. According to legend, Dr Dre discovered Em's demo tape on the floor of Interscope label chief Jimmy Iovine's garage, but the reality was that Eminem took second place in the freestyle category at 1997's Rap Olympics MC Battle in Los Angeles, and Iovine approached the rapper for a tape afterward. It wasn't until a month or two later that he played the tape for an enthusiastic Dre, who eagerly contacted Eminem.

The upshot was that Dre started recording "My Name Is". He agreed to produce Eminem's first album, and the pair released "Just Don't Give a Fuck" as a single to preview it. A reconciliation with his girlfriend led to Eminem and Kim getting married in the autumn of 1998. Interscope signed the rapper and prepared to give him a massive push on Dre's advice. That push put "My Name Is" into our lives. It's how you might care to remember him – a poptastically funky, funny-as-fuck introduction to his weirdly familiar world and the petulant intelligence that brutally crayoned in the vital, moral detail and Eminem's personal attitude to that world.

What's happened since is a little less palatable (and, musically, a damn sight less compulsive). Eminem is now pretty much rapper of choice for a generation of whining, spoilt adolescents with precious little concern for hip hop but plenty of concern for bitching about their easy lives every chance they get. It'd be a shame if Eminem simply becomes the voice of the middle-class, suburbanite, spoilt pre-teen, but it seems to be the way he wants to go. If we must, let's remember him before he got told he was the voice of the I-want-it-now generation. Before he got a little too comfortable with his potty mouth. Before he got a little too Elvis.

Strictly Business

(STRICTLY BUSINESS, FRESH/PRIORITY, 1988)

"Next time I'm on the scene. . . do not try to diss us/Keep your mouth suckered shut, because I'm strictly business. . . "

Dependability might seem a strange plus-point in the ever-changing world of rap, but for EPMD it was the guaranteed quality of their music that endeared them so much to the hearts of B-boys, so used to seeing rap acts blow up and disappear on the proceeds. The sample-heavy productions and nonchalant rap styles of Erick Sermon and Parrish Smith weren't gonna barrage down your door and take you over. Rather, the relationship you developed with EPMD was based on reliability and steadiness. Fundamentally, from 1988's *Strictly Business* to 1992's *Business Never Personal*, they were flawlessly good, unmissable leading lights of the east-coast underground. Superficially, EPMD were an unattractive proposition, their rhymes frequently inflected with all the passion and drama of a pair of robots. But it was precisely that dead-eyed cool that made them so damn good, such a remorseless, inarguable assault on your reservations.

Erick Sermon (aka Double E) and Parrish Smith (PMD) were both born in '68 and raised in the Long Island suburb of Brentwood, but their paths didn't cross for almost twenty years. Smith DJed for Rock Squad on a single for Tommy Boy before meeting Sermon in 1987.

Christening themselves, with typical, on-the-money obviousness, EPMD (Erick and Parrish Making Dollars), the duo recorded their debut, "It's My Thing", in three hours. Licensed to Chrysalis, then signed to Sleeping Bag/Fresh for their first album, *Strictly Business*, there was no immediate or discernible reason why it (and all the subsequent albums) became so enormously successful.

The industry always treated EPMD as a lucrative confusion, a band that sold steadily and hugely without anyone's permission, without much critical validation or media interest. The people EPMD sold to were beneath the radar, were the international brotherhood and sisterhood of hip hop fans who didn't subscribe to the fly-by-night nonsense pushed at us by an industry that never understood the music we loved. "Strictly Business", the title track of that debut, was typical – a stunning meld of beat and loop and rapping in the supercool monotone that had such a huge influence on Biggie and Nas, but without a spare, wasted moment, its truly inventive rhymes hidden by the lack of intonation. It was music that soundtracked life, made everything funky. By 1992, EPMD presided over an extended family dubbed the Hit Squad, including Redman, K-Solo and Das EFX. Their legacy to the future of hip hop is still with us, still mashing heads, still the B-boys' old familiar of choice.

ERIC B & RAKIM

(FOLLOW THE LEADER, UNI, 1988)

"Rap is Rhythm And Poetry, cuts create sound effects/You might catch up if you follow the records E. wrecks. . . "

We've all done it. In our bedrooms. Teenage boys. Y'know what they get up to. No, not that. I mean air-MCing. If teenage metal fans think they're unique in getting their hardcore jollies by widdling a tennis racket in the air along to Jimi, then they've clearly never been a fly on the wall of a B-boy's bedroom. It doesn't matter what you use. You can pretend you're holding a mic simply by clenching your fist (although a deodorant can would also suffice). Loose clothes are best. Some clear area is good, and a bed you can jump off is handy for those stage-diving encores. Crucial to the experience of air-MCing (which often crosses over with its air-DJing counterpart – and that's not just a euphemism for wanking, although the hand motions are fairly similar) is that you must know all the lyrics. Off by heart, and be able to drop them in the same accent and voice as your heroes. Draw the curtains. Lock, or block, the door. (Nothing's worse than being caught mid-flow by your mum – look, I'm not talking about wanking, OK?) Turn it up loud and press the fake steel mesh to your lips and go for it. Dead easy with a lot of hip hop in the late eighties, but Rakim made rapping along to records both a challenge and a training ground. No one sounded as cool at the time. Very few have sounded as cool since. Rakim is the original MC's MC.

Which might make you forget Eric B's contribution (and Rakim's assertions, since the duo split, that he was responsible for most of the music hasn't helped B's rep), but it was always the way the music seemed pulled along by Rakim's lyrics that made Eric B & Rakim one of the most thoughtful and effective duos in hip hop for a long time. By the time of *Follow The Leader*, the pair had been together for three years, having met in '85 when Eric was working for New York City radio station WBLS. They recorded a demo – "Eric B Is President" – which was released as a 45 on obscure Harlem indie label Zakia. Picked up by Fourth & Broadway and then leased to MCA after their debut album, Eric B & Rakim spent the next five years falling out with each other but developing a musical relationship that deepened over the course of three more albums, now considered essential to any hip hop collection.

The stunning, seamless meld they developed depended on sounds that seemed moulded, crafted, to the thoughts that would spill from Rakim's mind to his mouth. Here was no contrast of medium and message, here was no mere backing track for Rakim simply to coast upon. Here was music seemingly growing as each syllable was found, music that had no life before Rakim started talking. It was such a perfect blend of drama and dialogue it burned its own videos into your mind. Listening and rapping along, you could recast yourself in the most impossibly abstract visuals, feel the cameras swooping around you. And "Follow The Leader", from the duo's second LP, more than anything that'd come before it (the definitive *Paid In Full*) or after it (the next two tracks on the album were "Microphone Fiend" and "Lyrics Of Fury", worthy of books all of their own, and we're not even on to *Let The Rhythm Hit 'Em*

Rakim wonders if he's being outshone by his jewellery.

yet), was the most amazingly textured, heart-stoppingly cinematic track Eric B & Rakim ever made. Its influence, still, can't be underestimated, 'cos not only did Rakim show young rappers a revolutionary way of saying more by saying less, but the sound of "Follow The Leader" was perhaps the first time a lot of us realized that hip hop was head music, firing off its own storyboards through the sheer panoptic wow of its sound.

It's impossible to disassociate the elements in "Follow The Leader". Rakim's rhymes spill from street to stars to light years away to right in his heart within the space of single verses, all spoken and intoned with a calm, introspective clarity that sounded incredible in an age when Run DMC, LL Cool J and PE were bellowing their raps at top volume. The gliding, neon strings and propulsive, electro-fart bass combined to pull you and the track along on a ride that was going a little too fast for you to climb off, like a rollercoaster you regretted being tall enough to ride. In isolation, each part of "Follow The Leader" is awesome; heard simultaneously, it's one of the most ruthlessly organised headfucks that music has ever given us. Still a cave-in to the skull every time you hear it.

The most captivating duo in rap before Gang Starr, Eric B & Rakim.

Take A Personal

(DAILY OPERATION, CHRYSALIS, 1992)

"Bear in mind that you can't think as quick/So Premier drops a beat, for me to say verses to. . . "

Always seen as challenging, always seen as "seminal", always afforded maximum respect in hip hop circles, it almost seems dutiful to pay Gang Starr their due. What must never be forgotten, though, is that the reason GS are so respected is precisely why they've never achieved the crossover success lesser talents found so easily: Gang Starr, from the off, clearly never gave a fuck. About fame. About celebrity. About sales. About the rest of music. About the rest of hip hop. Gang Starr were committed to total exploration, both musically and lyrically, and never compromised the integrity of that vision for anybody: their lasting influence goes way beyond the mere details of Premo's revolutionary sonic experimentation, or Guru's laconic, sublimely cool vocalizing. They bequeath us an attitude of fearlessness and dedication to hip hop music that should be an inspiration to anyone picking up a mic or dropping a needle.

Sure, Gang Starr have always been peerless, but the two touchstone releases are still *Step In The Arena* (1991) and *Daily Operation* (1992) – the first because its use of jazz (in both music and lyrics) was the final word in the conversation started by Tribe's *The Low End Theory*, the second because it's an avant-garde yet hardcore masterpiece. This ruff-as-fuck slice of atonal funk mashes together freewheeling, Cecil Taylor-style anti-harmonies with a beat so murky it sounds like it's emanating from the depths of a Brooklyn sewer as De Niro's Travis Bickle rides by. It perfectly captures the moment where DJ Premier's production goes beyond the occasionally startling touches of *Step In The Arena* (the Band-sampling "Beyond Comprehension", the cine-funk of "Check The Technique") and finds its own bold, unique voice: a sound built out of seemingly avant-garde elements (music concrete, freejazz, drone noise) but put together with a natural, street-level genius that turns overthink into instinct, cleverness into brutality, and the conceptual into the actual.

You get the feeling with Premo, as you did with the Bomb Squad, that here is someone who sees his music before he makes it (and God knows what kind of nightmares "Soliloquy Of Chaos" came from), marshals his talent into the ability to transform the sonic chiaroscuros and smears of colour that music makes in his mind into a living breathing funky reality.

Following these two, undisputedly classic LPs, Premier became one of New York's most demanded producers, crafting hits for the city's finest MCs – The Notorious B.I.G., Nas, Jay-Z, KRS-One and more. For a while, it seemed that Gang Starr became somewhat of a side project for Premier and Guru, who both forged ahead with their respective solo careers. The *Hard To Earn* LP from

'94 and subsequent slabs of genius (*Moment Of Truth* in 1998, *The Ownerz* in 2003) were labelled comebacks simply because GS have always cared about quality and therefore wait until they have a filler-less masterpiece on their hands before they let us hear it. And, of course, Guru's contribution to the art of MCing can't be underestimated. He imposed on his listeners and his fans a kind of awed agitation, upping the ante on every other rapper who's come since and maintaining a totally honest, brilliantly imaginative relationship with the mic that educated, infuriated and captivated anyone in striking distance. Perhaps the best MC since Rakim. The best producer in hip hop history. A living model of hip hop perfection.

Mind Playing Tricks On Me

(WE CAN'T BE STOPPED, RAP-A-LOT, 1991)

"It was dark as fuck on the streets/My hands were all bloody, from punching on the concrete. . . "

Certain shadowy figures have had a huge effect on the development of hip hop culture even though their influence may be not directly as an artist but as a facilitator, a maker of connections. Often it's the most apparently unlikely people who make an impact. Look at how many times Rick Rubin, a Sonny Barger lookalike, long haired, noise-freak Slayer fan with a big-ass beard, has changed hip hop history. When the Geto Boys became one of the first gangster rap crews to be blocked from distributing their music, it was Rubin who arranged another distributor and released the Boys' debut album on his own Def American label. The controversy pre-dated similar legal problems thrown up two years later for Ice-T and 2 Live Crew.

The Geto Boys' first LP wouldn't have been a great loss to hip hop culture if it had never come out (how many songs about necrophilia do you need?) But if Bushwick Bill, Scarface and Willie D had consequently been prevented from bringing out their second album, featuring this stunning track, we'd have all been poorer for it. "Mind Playing Tricks On Me" is perhaps the most brutally effective and affecting, psychological diary rap has let us leaf through since Flash's "The Message".

The Geto Boys started with a completely different line-up. Jukebox, DJ Ready Red and Johnny C made up the bulk of the crew, with the pint-sized Bushwick Bill merely the dancer (formed in Houston, Texas, the Geto Boys clearly took their on-stage cues from local loons Butthole Surfers). When Johnny C and Jukebox quit, former Rap-A-Lot solo artists Scarface and Willie D were drafted in by the record company. In 1990, David Geffen refused to distribute *Grip It! On That Other Level* because the lyrics were so gloriously offensive (the refusal becoming a perfect marketing tool which Def American happily exploited when they remixed and repackaged the album as *The Geto Boys*, replete with the murder/necrophilia anthem "Mind Of A Lunatic").

The group left Geffen for Rap-A-Lot but were quickly involved in turmoil. Bushwick Bill was shot in the eye and partially blinded by his girlfriend after threatening their baby, an incident immortalized on the sleeve of *We Can't Be Stopped* with a gruesome shot of Bill being pushed through a hospital by Scarface and Willie D (one of the most memorable hip hop covers ever). The occasional moments of insight revealed on The Geto Boys (such as "Life In The Fast Lane") reached a stunning, revelatory denouement on *We Can't Be Stopped*, especially on "Mind Playing Tricks On Me". Over crepuscular, neon G-Funk, the song details paranoia with a fearless, scarcely therapeutic anger that chills the bones. Scarface talks of not being able to leave his room for fear of his nightmares of the devil coming true, Willie D of the cars he feels are tailing him, Bushwick Bill of the "seven-foot nigga" in his dreams who simply "disappears" when he swings at him. It unfolds like a crack-ravaged frightmare of half-seen shadows and peripheral phantoms, forever lurking in the Geto Boys' imaginations, perhaps genuinely lurking in the mental murk to pull them into total insanity. It's a rap record where the voices offer no relief, no conviction, only the dread possibility that the things they're talking about are all too real, could step beyond the shadows and into real life. As such, it perfectly detailed the socio-psychological damage crack and a decade of Reaganomics had accomplished in America's underbelly. Hear it, and feel the freeze.

GRANDMASTER FLASH & THE FURIOUS FIVE

The Message

(THE MESSAGE, SUGAR HILL, 1982)

"Don't push me cos I'm close to the edge/I'm trying not to lose my head. . . "

Everything led up to "The Message" and then everything led away from it. But then, would hip hop as we know it even exist without Grandmaster Flash – perhaps the first name any of us ever associated with rap music? His influence on the subject of this book is so vast on all fronts he gives the lie to the idea that no one is bigger than rap, that hip hop would've survived without any of its founding participants. You just can't imagine rap being the same without Flash, either musically or in the subjects it could address. What Flash did reminds you that when hip hop kicked off, it didn't know where to go, didn't have a clue what it could become, was fundamentally an underground, artistic movement without a manifesto, without self-knowledge, creating a new sound as it went along, with all the playfulness and innocence that that implies. To turn something so seemingly up-for-grabs into a cogent movement, an idea that could change the world, takes people willing to see into the future, people able to impose their will on something nobody felt they could ever control. Rap could've disappeared off the face of the planet, got swallowed up by funk or electro or soul. It could've simply become another technique for black pop to use, rather than the resistant, anti-pop voice of a people for whom shiny, happy "urban" music wouldn't suffice. It was visionaries – weird, obsessive, music junkies like Flash, like Herc, like Bambaataa (the holy trinity of hip hop) that refused to let rap exist as a mere fad. We owe them big time.

Flash was a pivotal force in early hip hop and like so many other pivotal forces, he came from the South Bronx (and like so many, he was born elsewhere, in Flash's case Barbados). Born Joseph Saddler, he studied hard at technical school and spent his spare time at DJ parties thrown by early movers

One of the most brilliantly innocent shots in hip hop history. The Magnificent Six take on the world.

like DJ Flowers, Maboya and Peter Jones, who took him under his wing. Flash devised a way of combining Jones' timing on the decks with Kool Herc's musical knowledge. In the early seventies, Saddler discovered how to segue records together without missing a beat, finding the "break" and repeating it. Dedicated to the point of fanaticism, frantic, a bedroom lunatic who just happened to be on the verge of one of the most important discoveries in hip hop history, Saddler spent a year in his 167th Street apartment experimenting with record decks. He adapted what he'd seen Herc doing at the Hevalo, using two turntables spinning the same record. He'd pause one, overlay the break, and then switch mixing channels interminably until he had a whole flow of pure beats, always having to spin back each break to exactly the right point before he switched channels.

Though Herc had pioneered breaks, and sampling, Flash turned those into an art, a skill that looked as visual as it sounded. He also made the crucial discovery that "flash" though his deck abilities were, they weren't enough to hold a crowd in performance. Doubtless hugely influenced by U-Roy, and the ragamuffin roots virtually all pioneers of rap were steeped in, he decided to invite a vocalist to share the stage with him, first Lovebug Starski and then Keith Wiggins. Wiggins would come to be known as Cowboy within Grandmaster Flash's Furious Five, in the process becoming one of the first ever MCs (alongside Herc's MC, Coke La Rock), dropping rhymes to accompany Flash's turntable pyrotechnics.

Flash carried on performing at block parties and park parties for some time, illegally hooking up his sound system to intercepted mains cables until the police arrived. It was Ray Chandler who saw commercial potential in this essentially underground phenomenon (block parties were always free) and asked Flash to allow him to promote him, charge an entrance fee, see who'd be willing to pay. Flash didn't believe anyone would pay to see him spin records. But he agreed.

In the process he put together one of the first hip hop groups. The strong line-up of local talent he recruited included Grandmaster Melle Mel, Kid Creole and Cowboy to form Grandmaster Flash & The Three MCs. Two further rappers, Duke Bootee and Kurtis Blow, subsequently joined but were replaced eventually by Rahiem and Scorpio. The Zulu Tribe was inaugurated to act as security at events.

With Flash making this new rap format (ones and twos and a mic) more popular, rival MCs sprang up to take their mentor and each other on. These fledgling "battles" won equipment for the winning participants – the losers would see their gear rehabilitated to more talented crews. All this owed a great deal to the rich history of Jamaican, sound-system owners like Duke Reid and Coxsone Dodd. Flash, Herc and Bambaataa would hide their records, rub off the labels, like King Tubby and U-Roy would.

Similarly, all were involved in a revolution in music that could be summed up as creativity through destruction. Just as Tubby and Roy would break down records' constituent elements to pioneer the new sound of dub, so Flash and Herc would smash the authorial bounds and internal integrity of a track to create what would be called hip hop. Where dub attacked roots and ska, hip hop would attack funk and the disco it despised so much.

The Furious Five made their debut proper in late '76. Soon after, their first record, "Superrappin'", came out on Enjoy and instantly became a totemic anthem for the hip hop community (as it wasn't yet known). "We Rap Mellow" and "Flash To The Beat" were other records featuring Flash that failed to cross over. It wasn't until Joe Robinson Jr of Sugar Hill Records bought the Furious Five's contract from Enjoy that Flash would start making the waves his innovations deserved.

Robinson had seen Flash in action at the Bronx's Disco Fever (often called "hip hop's first home", although rival clubs the T-Connection and Harlem World could also lay claim to that title), and signed him as soon as he could. Singles like "Freedom" and "Birthday Party" made little impact, but "The Adventures Of Grandmaster Flash On The Wheels Of Steel" was like nothing (and everything)

else anyone had ever heard – the first rap record defiantly to use samples in a dominant, chaotic fashion (Chic, Blondie and Queen rattled by at the speed of light) and a sonic *tour de force* that put Flash firmly at the top of the DJ game.

"The Message" was brought to an unconvinced Furious Five by Joe Robinson (who'd co-written it with Duke Bootee); the resultant single went platinum in a month. While it was busy becoming the biggest-selling rap single of that time, it was also pushing the boundaries of what hip hop could talk about, the musical territory hip hop could reach into, fundamentally realigning the entire, future history of black music. An apocalyptic testimony that interweaved social upheaval, political history, personal paranoia and global collapse into one coherent narrative – in one fell swoop of bass and blast-beats, "The Message" transformed hip hop, transcending the music's party-

Who these days would have the balls to wear this? Sly Stone finds a couple of friends in Fire Island.

down origins and giving it a new future of social critique and personal exploration. Flash would go on to make other great records, and he would be among the first of hip hop's practitioners to learn about the ravages the business would put rap through before it got its due, but "The Message" remains the birth-joint of pretty much everything that's happened since in hip hop, the first rap record to stop the boasting and turn its gaze inward and outward, a record that still sounds as fearless and earth-shaking as it did on first contact.

GRAVE-DIGGAZ

1-800 Suicide

(NIGGAMORTIS, GEE STREET, 1994)

"The only one to escape was number Six, he went home/Sat in the tub and slit his wrists, yeah, more graves to dig. . . "

Of course, "horrorcore", as the crush of hardcore rap and gothic imagery that Gravediggaz invented was christened by the press, was always a joke, a non-event, a journalistic phrase in search of a place of real reference. I use it now with some fondness, partly for the way it instantly recalls the Gravediggaz' unblinking and ridicule-tempting emergence into the light of day but also because it really does sum up the unique nature of what occurred on their debut LP *Niggamortis* (called *Six Feet Deep* by nervous American distributors). A minor hit, whose singles grazed the charts, the album had a unique appeal that rested on Gravediggaz' timeliness. After grunge had reinvigorated rock by tuning down its positivist elements and focusing wholly on its nihilism (the "yes" at rock'n'roll's heart silenced in favour of the "no" that always informed it), so Gravediggaz brought a gloom and despondency to hardcore hip hop that it never had before. These weren't rappers defiantly standing up to death (other people) or to life (other people) – this was rappers shutting all other people out before gleefully submitting themselves to fantasies of their own doom and global decay that film director George Romero would cream over (see also Chino XL and Group Home).

The mastermind of the group, The Undertaker, was better known as Stetsasonic's Prince Paul (born Paul Huston): the other members included Rzarector (The RZA of Wu-Tang Clan), Grym Reaper (Poetic from Too Poetic), and Gatekeeper (Frukwan, born Arnold Hamilton, also ex-Stetsasonic). But the crew's supergroup status didn't stop them pushing out into bold new areas of hip hop territory on *Niggamortis*.

It's Prince Paul's clear frustration at the collapse of his Doo Dew label that accounts for the album's sheer darkness, and blackest of all is "1–800 Suicide", a tormented tale of death wishes coming true that still makes you wince every time its Hammond-in-hell riff comes blowing in. As such a bizarrely pan-genre act, mixing the sonics of hardcore rap with the imagery of death metal, Gravediggaz made a lot of converts to hip hop in the mid-nineties, especially among metal fans and rockers. Those converts would go on to make Eminem a star and Necro an underground hero. Many of the backpacking generation started here.

Fangs for the memories. Gravediggaz circa the release of 'Niggamortis'.

L'Empire De Côté Obscur

(L'ECOLE DU MICRO D'ARGENT, 1996 VIRGIN)

"Pour les rebelles la force est trop forte
Je balaie les petits Ewoks comme le vent balaie les feuilles mortes"

Despite French hip hop's predominantly black and Arab following, hip hop is used by French groups as a means of forging unity across racial lines. Unlike their American counterparts, French rap groups are often multiracial. The Marseilles-based rap crew IAM (Imperial Asiatic Men), who use Pharaonic nicknames (Kheops, Akhenaton, Imhotep and Divin Khepren), are actually of Malian, Algerian, Spanish, and Italian origin. And while they celebrate humanity's origins in Africa, the motherland ("la terre-mere"), and condemn slavery and apartheid, IAM stress the importance of racial tolerance and unity, and on the track "Blanc et Noire" compare Louis Farrakhan to France's radically conservative messenger of hate, Jean-Marie le Pen of the National Front.

Critiques of global capitalism (they're very fond of bitching about "ce putain d'tat" ("this f--king state")) have not prevented IAM from becoming "guerrilla capitalists" and establishing a record label, Cot' Obscur, which has produced gold albums for Fonky Family and Se Oeil. Self-sufficient independent non-American rap culture, as promoted by labels like Cot' Obscur or England's phenomenal Big Dada and YNR records, is the creative launchpad from which hip hop's next stage of development will be launched. And this volume will merely be an addendum to the World Encyclopedia of hip hop that's yet to be written.

ICE CUBE

The Wrong Nigga To Fuck Wit

(DEATH CERTIFICATE, FOURTH & BROADWAY, 1991)

"Mess with the Cube, you get punked quick/Pig, cos I'm the wrong nigga to fuck wit!"

Where's he gone? Cube was such a central figure in the rap mythology of the late eighties and early nineties, his current absence from our radar seems not just curious but potentially unhealthy for such a seeker of the spotlight, such a commandeer of hip hop's centre-stage. Perhaps it was Cube's restlessness that undid him: from his early days in NWA through to his attempt to ride Dre's G-Funk wave on 1994's *Lethal Injection*, Cube was always willing to change his focus, politically and musically, and that led to the idea (promulgated by Cube-haters such as Cypress Hill) that he was a fly-by-night rapper, in it for the money, who changed tack every time he felt the cash-flow drying up. His forays into movies didn't help. He used to make movies with his mouth, with his music.

Born Oshea Jackson in the late sixties in Crenshaw, South Central, Cube came from a relatively well-to-do background, already implying that the gangster pose he adopted for NWA was something of an affectation. Penning "Boyz-n-The-Hood" (later recorded by Eazy-E) at the age of 16, and bringing "Dopeman" and "8 Ball" to the NWA setlist, he'd leave at the tail-end of 1989 amid thinly veiled attacks on NWA's Jewish manager, Jerry Heller.

His debut album, *Amerikkka's Most Wanted*, racked neatly beside Public Enemy's *Fear Of A Black Planet* set in 1990 as most B-boys' agit-prop of choice (the Bomb Squad production and guest spots from PE's Chuck D and Flavor Flav helped too).

But beyond the political posturing, the virulent nastiness that made Cube so addictive found its full flowering on his second album. *Death Certificate* was to relish, being at the time one of vilest hip hop albums money could buy, a sexist, racist, homophobic assault on liberal values and a white world Cube clearly despised (while selling to in vast amounts).

What always struck you about Cube was how you couldn't tell if he was growing up in public or simply trying to please everybody. He certainly got himself heard by as many people as possible on rock tours, festivals and Lollapalooza bills that had produced such similar, crossover success for Ice-T. *Death Certificate* perfectly caught the dichotomy between Cube's NWA gangsta past and his self-modelled emergence into a proud, Nation Of Islam future. Every time he dropped conscious rhymes, you felt the righteousness was a little too violently expressed to be genuine, his violence a little too simplistically righteous to be based in any reality he'd known.

So while we could diss Cube for his bandwagon jumping, we could all secretly admire him for his self-transforming ability to fit in everywhere, to play whatever role was demanded of him.

This was rap as wish fulfilment, affording Cube the ability to be both a dirty, low-down sonofabitch ("Givin' Up The Nappy Dugout" and "You Can't Fade Me", with its delightful let's-kick-our-pregnant-girlfriend shtick) and a proud black man going about the business of empowering his people ("I Wanna Kill Sam").

The Predator, the album that followed *Death Certificate*, was way more successful in portraying the positive side of what Cube had to say (openers "When Will They Shoot?" and "Wicked", together with "It Was A Good Day" remain unforgettable) but "The Wrong Nigga To Fuck Wit" encapsulates perfectly the contradictions that made Cube so listenable as an artist, so readable as a liar. An MC we all adored that none of us believe in anymore.

ICE-T
Original Gangster

(ORIGINAL GANGSTER, SYNDICATE/SIRE, 1991)

"I use my pad and pen and my lyrics break out mad/I try to write about fun and the good times but. . . "

For a figure so often held up as a star in the hip hop firmament, you'd be hard pressed to find a hip hop fan who'll admit they ever loved Ice-T. The qualities that endeared him to so many people who weren't solely into hip hop are exactly the qualities that make B-boys suspect him, traduce him as an interloper and an outsider and condemn him forthwith. True, the patronizing way T was treated by the mainstream press did him no favours among the hardcore heads: he was always seen as "surprisingly" articulate and intelligent, suggesting that most rappers were monosyllabic mouth-breathers at best. His willingness to reach out beyond the hip hop fanbase and embrace the metal and rock worlds which fired his imagination and sometimes his music was seen as a traitorous (and essentially pointless) attempt to hide his own lack of hardcore kudos. In so many ways, so much of what Ice-T did after he became famous has, in retrospect, trashed any fond memory his more avowedly hardcore beginnings might have engendered.

Well, fuck all that. And fuck elitist B-boys. Ice-T will always be a star. He will always be a model of how to stay a B-boy, stay paid and stay ahead of the game. His best music still stands up as some of the finest west-coast rap of all time. Over three incredible albums, he was one of the most consistently absorbing artists in music, full stop. The paths he took, the bridges he built between hip hop and alternative music are still being travelled today, still making connections whose resonance remains undimmed. Ice-T's the fuckin' man. Don't let hip hop snobs fool ya.

Ice-T (aka Tracey Marrow) was born in Newark, New Jersey. When he was a child, his parents died in a car accident and he moved to California. Obsessed with rap at Crenshaw High School in South Central LA, he took his name from Iceberg Slim, ex-pimp turned novelist and public speaker. Teenage Tracey memorized lines from Slim's writings, reciting them for classmates.

Having left high school, he recorded several undistinguished 12" singles in the early eighties. He also appeared in the low-budget, hip hop films *Rappin'*, *Breakin'* and *Breakin' II: Electric Boogaloo*, just looking for an opening, a chance at something. Finally, he landed a major-label record deal with Sire in 1987 and recorded his debut album, *Rhyme Pays*, with DJ Aladdin and producer Afrika Islam. It was a solid-gold seller and a party masterpiece. Still, when Ice recorded a track called "Colors" and an album, *Power*, for his own label, Rhyme Syndicate, in 1988 he hit new heights. A definitively LA-sounding suite of hi-rolling grace and biting social critique, *Power* was gangsta rap a year before LA would explode with it. By the time NWA had arrived at the place where *Power* was, Ice-T was already up and running, miles away.

He released a stunning album, *The Iceberg: Freedom Of Speech. . . Just Watch What You Say*, in '89, and it established him as a true, hip hop superstar, matching Sabbath-mashing, full-tilt funk music with fierce, intelligent narratives, guest spots from no less than Jello Biafra and a vital, impassioned voice on the storm clouds of censorship that were gathering on rap's horizon. In Ice's future was Body Count, "Cop Killer", movie roles, Lollapalooza and wars with Charlton Heston. *Original Gangster* captures him in between *The Iceberg. . .* and that first Body Count album – a man sure of his identity but dimly aware that some grim, gruesome, gnarly shit is gonna kick off for him if he keeps opening that righteous mouth.

Original Gangster is still one of the highlights of nineties, west-coast rap, way more musically diverse than all of the predictable hardcore LA was coughing up at the time. It's an album that stands as Ice's masterpiece because it contains the myriad elements and personas (the metal geek, the hi-rolling pimp, the street thug, the aspirational intellectual) that sprinkled Ice with such compulsive stardust.

The title track is simply the hardest, funkiest, most instantaneously head-caving slab of greatness that the record had to offer. I defy you not to snap your neck. I defy anyone hearing it to question Ice-T's appearance in any hip hop fan's dream team. And for all you snobs? Y'mama's got gold feet growing out of her titties. Bitch fell down, kept running.

JAY-Z

Bring It On

(REASONABLE DOUBT, ROC-A-FELLA, 1996)

"Do the knowledge, do the few dollars, I'm due to demolish/Crews Brooklyn through Hollis to a hood near you, what the fuck. . . "

So, the long-awaited *The Black Album* came and went, and with it went the career of the most prominent nu-skool, Nuyorican superstar of the late nineties and new millennium. Jay-Z as a commercial fact can easily dominate you into a critical silence simply with his crazy figures, impossible numbers. The dizzying volume of records he's sold, the staggering amount of hits that his albums seem to generate, can obliterate all sense when it comes to talking of Jay's musical worth.

Making his debut in 1996, Jay-Z went on to create the Roc-A-Fella Records dynasty by dint of his untrammelled hunger to be the biggest rap star on the planet. Roc-A-Fella, the label he began with Damon Dash, has become its own marketing tool, spawning a clothing line, a deep roster of talent (Beanie Sigel, Cam'ron, M.O.P.) and producers (Just Blaze, Kanye West), cross-country hip hop tours, liquor brands, footwear shops and even Hollywood films. With his franchise in such a determinedly meteoric ascendant since the beginning, it's easy to forget what ostensibly got Jay where he is. His music. His music has soundtracked black America for half a decade with an endless parade of singles ensuring his omnipresence on urban radio and video.

He's stayed at the top with suburbanite MTV junkies and street-level hip hop fans. Any rivals (notably Nas) have been knocked out the water, and Jay's Roc-A-Fella clique can claim unchecked power over hip hop right now. Not just 'cos Jay's always worked with the hottest producers (Premo, Clark Kent, Teddy Riley, the Trackmasters, Erick Sermon, Timbaland, The Neptunes) and the hottest rappers (Biggie, Ja Rule, DMX, Ludacris, Missy Elliott) but because he's been a model of focused megalomania at a time (post-Biggie and Tupac)

where rap needed order and tyrannical, commercial domination by someone inside the B-boy mentality.

Jay's early, stamping ground was The Marcy Projects – a housing complex and Brooklyn ghetto. Family dysfunction meant that he, like many rappers in the making, had to find a new community to accept him. Sometimes criminal (he street-hustled from his early teens), sometimes artistic, Jay learned his way around the rap industry from New York rapper Jaz-O while also filling in for a little-known crew called Original Flavor.

Rather than sign with an established company, Jay-Z decided to form his own label with friends Damon Dash and Kareem "Biggs" Burke. The fledgling Roc-A-Fella secured a distribution deal with Priority Records (and, later, Def Jam), and Jay's debut set, *Reasonable Doubt*, came out in 1996. It's still his crowning achievement, possessing a depth and maturity that was, curiously, not apparent on later records.

Reasonable Doubt is a nostalgic album – nostalgic not only for Jay's own hustling days but also for the old-skool, gangsta mindset Jay could see was on its last legs. "Bring It On" was the stand-out track, a thumping, confrontational gem which partnered Jay with one-time benefactor Big Jaz. Listening to it now, it's awesome to be reminded of just what a talented MC Jay is, and just how much of that talent has been obscured by the sheer, crazy, rush of what's happened to him since. Bigger-selling albums and bigger confrontations would be waiting for him, but *Reasonable Doubt* remains Jay's most potent contribution to the hip hop cannon.

Of course, Z's vaunting ambition was always apparent. "I didn't come into the rap game just to be a rapper, I came to be a CEO," he said after releasing *Reasonable Doubt*. "I didn't want to go into the movie business just to be an actor. I want to write scripts, produce, direct. I want it all." It took him half a

The last millenium's last King of Rap, Jay-Z bringin' it on.

decade, but he got it, just, by the skin of his teeth – then found out quickly that it's tense at the top, and that even the most potent voice in hip hop has to bite his lip now and then. Put on probation for three years in 2001 after admitting to stabbing producer Lance Rivera, Jay miraculously kept his nose clean as, around him, all hell broke loose.

By 2003, the rumour mill was chattering non-stop about the chaos going down at Roc-A-Fella Records, Jay reportedly falling out massively with co-CEO Damon Dash over the label's new, multi-genre direction while himself running foul of disses (and a planned mock-lynching) from arch-rivals Nas (who called Jigga "Gay-Z"), 2003's biggest rap whipping-boy Ja Rule, Irv Gotti and the whole Murder Inc stable, and even Roc-A-Fella's newest signing, Cam'ron. With Roc-roster star Beanie Sigel facing an attempted murder charge over a Philadelphia nightclub shooting, Jay reportedly not on speaking terms with Dash (the signing of ODB over Jay's head seems to have been the final straw) and even Jay's barber getting in on the action (he went psycho and shot three people), the collapse of the Roc-A-Fella partnership seems like an inevitability now that Jay has retired from rap altogether.

Predictions are that Dash and Z will each be given their own label by Def Jam's Lyor Cohen once the divvying-up of the Roc-A-Fella empire is over. For all his pull, industry insiders have been speculating that beneath the cool veneer, the most gorgeous girlfriend on the planet (Beyoncé Knowles, lucky fucker!) and the safe knowledge that, unlike Dash, he's never required liposuction, Jay faces the most insecure period of his career thus far.

All of which Shawn Carter (Jay's real name) can legitimately not give a tinker's cuss about. One can't help feeling that he'll respond to this madness with simply more lunacy of his own. Let's not forget how he drew an end to the Nas beef, which had seen Nas drop "Ether" in response to Jigga's "Takeover" on *The Blueprint*. Jay shot back, viciously, with "Super Ugly", in which he not only implied that NBA star Allen Iverson had enjoyed the company of the mother of Nas' daughter, but also offered lurid details of his own alleged adventures with her – "Left condoms on your baby seat" being perhaps being the choicest line. But even if Jay's never heard of again (unlikely) he can lay claim to being the harsh ruler hip hop needed in a time of crisis, the man who showed the rest of hip hop just how big this thing called rap could get. We're all spectators in Jay's world right now. When this king gets unseated is when rap's history takes another turn.

**Jay-Z in his regulation East Coast
hardcore uniform.**

JERU THE DAMAJA

Come Clean

(THE SUN RISES IN THE EAST, FULL FREQUENCY/PGD, 1994)

"When I'm bustin' ass and breakin' backs, inhale the putrified aroma/Breathe too deep and you'll wind up coma-tose. . . "
Proof that hip hop isn't always about what it lets in, the connections it can make with other music and cultures, and its openness. Sometimes hip hop is about being enclosed, locked in and off on your own shit, shutting out the rest of the world. If you drop "Come Clean" in a hip hop club any time, anywhere, you can be guaranteed the place will go wild. But when it came out on twelve in the UK, it was the kind of record you lived in for a month, kept to yourself, zeroed in on as all else failed you.

It was the kind of record you teased yourself about buying. You'd walk in the shop at a distressingly early hour (having spent all night counting up your coppers) and act as if you didn't know what you were going to get. You'd amble around the racks, half-heartedly pretending to look for something, and then you couldn't stand the anticipation any longer. You found "Come Clean", bought it, sat down on a bench and smelt it, peeled off the plastic and smelt that too, took it home, played it, and realised you were gonna have to change your mental landscape, rearrange your internal geography. It came along at just the right time. In 1995, there was something uncommonly friendly about rap to traditionally hip hop-unfriendly ears (the press, the media, white rock fans) – a combination of the new-found, radio-friendly professionalism of west-coast gangsta rap and its lyrical appeal to all the worse stereotypes of white imagination. In such a frustratingly wrong-headed atmosphere (where rap was finally getting its dues but at its creative nadir), tracks like "Come

Clean" and Mobb Deep's "Survival Of The Fittest" were a welcome, icy blast from the east coast, reminders that hip hop could still sound like nothing else and talk in a language not easily decipherable or instantaneously understandable. "Come Clean" is a hostile record. In all senses.

Lyrically, you could tell Jeru emerged from the Gang Starr stable (his guest spots on *Daily Operation* were a tip-off to a major talent), but by the time he came to record his solo debut, *The Sun Rises In The East*, he seemed even further out than the Guru in his syntactical leaps, his dizzying ability to conflate aggression, universality and political consciousness into single songs, single rhymes, single lines. "Come Clean" is the unpackings of a mind at the end of its tether but possessed of a frightening intellect, a mind that could fly to all points in the cosmos seemingly at will, able to slip between time, across the ages like some omnipotent, hip hop timelord.

Similarly, the loop Premo cooked up for him on his first transmission seemed both ancient and futuristic, an echoed, African drumbeat thumping out a rhythm you couldn't imagine anyone could rap to, let alone base a track on. In Premo's hands, the beat shape-shifted, suggested melodies of its own, pulsed throughout "Come Clean" like the first heartbeat of the cosmos and the last echoes of a disappearing planet. The scratched drop-ins served to take the music away from both past and present and locate an Afro-futurist mindset firmly in the here and now. At a time when rap was losing its relationship with its past, losing sight of its future, "Come Clean" made hip hop sound like the oldest sound on earth and the only sound that would ever matter. A reinvigoration of the faith. Word.

JUNGLE BROTHERS

Because I Got It Like That

(STRAIGHT OUT THE JUNGLE, WARLOCK, 1988)

"You've got a lot of talent, but you fail to see
You paid for yours, I got mine for free. . . "

hip hop fans are a funny breed. While the music they love frequently points its way in all directions, and they investigate those trails forthwith (a lot of us can trace every record we own back to our first PE or Quest album), if something is given to them that calls itself hip hop, it better damn well be hip hop and nothing else, or they'll build up a chagrined chip on their shoulder that'll never fall off.

Jungle Brothers predated the jazz-rap inflections of De La and Tribe, embraced Afrocentric perspectives, forayed into house, came back – and every step of the way, they were rejected by both hip hop and mainstream audiences. It was the slipperiness that rubbed people up the wrong way, but it was that same restlessness that now makes albums like *Straight Out The Jungle* and *Done By The Forces Of Nature* so compulsive. It's as if, even before they became major figures in hip hop history, the JBs were attempting to sabotage any attempt you might make to shore them up as veterans, old dependables, even though in a lot of ways, they were perhaps the most traditional group in rap at the time, certainly the band at most pains to point out their debt to what came before them. In the whole Native Tongue stable, the Jungle Brothers were the most isolated crew and that isolation made record companies worry. Which meant that for a frustratingly big chunk of the JBs' career, the crew were waiting around for the industry to grow balls big enough to deal with these mavericks properly – a shame that can only be corrected by people digging these albums out now.

The JBs gave a sound and a name to the whole Native Tongue movement, but they took their cues from two sources. James Brown gave them their initials and the absolute roots of their music – they set about tearing his legacy to shreds and reconfiguring it for their own ends with a dedication and knowledge that clearly showed true fandom at work. Afrika Bambaataa was the other influence, both in the Jungle Brothers' genre-hopping glee and in the politics that informed all their work. They, like Bambaataa, would see their role fundamentally as one of education and uplift, seeking to enhance the lives of black men and women by teaching them about their role in history generally and African culture specifically.

So far so worthy so fucking dull: what made the JBs actually listenable was the slapdash craziness of their music. They were among the first crews to start paying homage to other hip hop, not just old funk, and when they did turn their wacky, wrecking skills to records you knew, they threw them down with such demented speed and breathless passion you had to be pulled along, even as you were spotting the joins. "Because I Got It Like That" comes about three-quarters of the way through *Straight Out The Jungle* and it's so simply effective it seems to seal up the whole record – just a big-assed Sly Stone beat thrown down by DJ Sammy B, with Afrika Baby Bam and Mike G live-freestyling over the top. Why the Jungle Brothers never got their due remains one of the enduring mysteries of hip hop history. Or rather, it's an object lesson in the values of blissful ignorance.

Beatnik b-boys par excellence, the
Jungle Brothers.

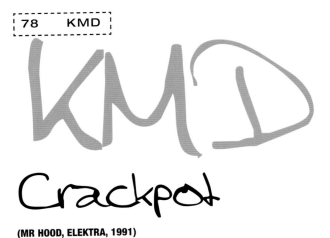

Crackpot

(MR HOOD, ELEKTRA, 1991)

"I first met Crackpot in like Head Starts/And then I knew he wasn't too head smart cuz I scribbled in art. . . "

I feel like I should declare an interest here, so intimately have I felt connected with this record over the years. "Crackpot" and, more specifically, *Mr Hood*, the album it comes from, is perhaps my favourite hip hop record of all time. It's followed me from the end of my childhood through to the beginnings of my middle age and it's always been a record I've wanted to hear above all others. It's a record I get evangelical about to people who've never bought a hip hop album in their lives. It's a record whose absence in any hip hop fan's collection sends me into fits of exaggerated disgust. For many, by the time it'd come out, *Mr Hood* was simply an interesting adjunct to the Daisy Age story, a fairly good mix of beats from contemporary, hot producers like Pete Nice and Dante Ross, a fairly successful but amateurish concept LP. I'd call it one of the greatest, lost masterpieces of American art in the twentieth century. I'm not sure if it represents simply the highpoint of late eighties/early nineties hip hop production, but it represents perhaps the most human, touching outcrop of that golden age.

KMD made records that always seemed to need catching up with: on first hearing, you couldn't quite get all the mad detail and delicious refraction that they seemed to be able to capture on wax. It's only after a little growing up that you realise what hooked you wasn't merely the incredible sound of Mr Hood, it was the heart, the living, breathing reality of the record that transmitted other lives, other thoughts and other realities directly to you uncut, unsimplified and pure, and as immeasurably complex as any human communication can be. And the clarity of that communication doesn't succumb to the rose-tints of retrospect, doesn't lose its power now that we can place KMD in a lineage. Rather, the clarity creates its own lineage, creates its own space, and puts KMD out on their own in any hip hop fan's imagination. They were perhaps the unluckiest genii rap ever gave us.

MC Serch of 3rd Bass discovered MC Zevlove X, DJ Subroc and Onyx The Birthstone Kid and made them a key element in 3rd Bass's RIF production roster. From the low-key, brilliant sleeve to the music on the record, *Mr Hood* was a detonation of stereotypes from the off. Letting their wit and sense of wonder push through political correctness and conservative revisionism, KMD shone a bright light of cynicism and idealism through the burning issues of

1991 – none of which would've made *Mr Hood* such a potent work if the music hadn't been so instantaneously dazzling. Primed by De La and Tribe, many of us discovered that *Mr Hood* had taken Prince Paul's cartoon lunacy into whole new areas. Here was a scattershot vision of pop culture and high conceptual art that simmered with a street-level honesty no one else had ever attained. For a record so crammed to bursting with sounds from all over the shop and a pure Looney-Tunes mentality, everything was carefully marshalled around the messages KMD were trying to transmit. So the threadbare concept of the happenings around a barbershop and KMD's humorous encounters with a straight-talking, English-language-course-speaking *Mr Hood*, attained the feel of a growing revelation rather than a steadily thinning metaphor.

"Crackpot" is the first real non-skit track on the album, and hearing it now you feel a rumble in your guts, knowing that the feast is about to get underway, or maybe it's butterflies of sadness knowing that though the beginnings of the KMD story were so hopeful, things would end up so badly. Follow-up LP *Black Bastards* was destroyed by Elektra over cover art that featured a "sambo" cartoon being hung by a noose – an image lambasted and utterly misunderstood by *Billboard* chart manager Terri Rossi. With Time Warner buzzing on the heightened paranoia created by Ice-T's "Cop Killer" controversy, KMD were dropped wholesale by the label, even though the band were willing to discuss changes to the cover, even though DJ Subroc, Zevlove X's brother, was killed in a car crash shortly after the album's completion. It's a shitty business, and the treatment of KMD is to its eternal shame. Get *Mr Hood* and quickly realize why.

KOOL G RAP & DJ POLO

Streets Of New York

(WANTED: DEAD OR ALIVE, COLD CHILLIN', 1990)

"Blind man plays the sax/A tune called "The Arms on My Moms Show Railroad Tracks". . . "

So, what is hardcore? Not a rhetorical question. Nobody knows. Unlike punk, where "hardcore" could be specifically applied to a certain offshoot of the movement that had its own history, bands, mode of dress etc, pinpointing exactly what constitutes hardcore hip hop, exactly what marks out its "hardcoreness" is a lot more difficult, a lot more illusory, and a lot more all-inclusive – every rapper on earth likes to think he's hardcore. Still, if you really want to hunt down the hardcore impulse, trace its origins and see what a huge influence the hardcore mentality has had on current hip hop, you'd be hard-pressed to find a better lesson than progressing straight on from Run DMC to BDP to Kool G Rap & DJ Polo.

Protégés of Marley Marl who never got the profile other Marl-ingénues received, Queens-born-and-bred Nathaniel Wilson (Kool G) and DJ Polo made three albums ('89's *Road To The Riches*, '90's *Wanted: Dead Or Alive* and '92's *Live And Let Die*) that pretty much stand alone as the lodestone of hardcore hip hop. Hugely underrated at the time, only now really being recognized as the seminal influence they were, it's clear that rappers as diverse as Nas, Raekwon, Jay-Z and Biggie all took their cues from the formulation Rap and Polo worked out over a decade ago. What G excelled at was the street narrative, stories that started out like a half-heard, second-hand conversation but ended with you and G together fighting for your life. Tracks like "Poison", "Men At Work" and "Truly Yours" benefited hugely from Marl's raw-yet-lethal production and by the time of *Wanted'*, though Marl had departed the desk (Eric B and Large Professor more than ably filled the seat), Kool G really had become the Kool Genius of rap he promised he would, the fully-rounded rapper that the debut single "I'm Fly" (and a blazing cameo on the Juice Crew's unforgettable "The Symphony") had hinted at so tantalizingly a full five years previously.

"Streets Of New York" is one of the most compellingly realistic urban narratives hip hop ever gave us, cutting from Kool's real, tangible experience on those streets into areas of general street philosophy with all the careless, chaotic conviction of a real conversation with somebody who'd ordinarily scare you out of your skin. It was like getting New York described to you not by an observer or an artist but by a willing, and potentially, extremely dodgy participant; the music felt like the rattle and rush of a Brooklyn-bound D-train, the clamour of rush-hour traffic, the heat and distended dread of the wrong street corner.

The next and final LP, *Live And Let Die*, was junked by Warners when they saw the sleeve – Kool and Polo in balaclavas, feeding raw steak to a pair of rotweillers while two white guys stand on chairs in the background wearing matching nooses – and an Ice Cube cameo sent the censorship lobby into even more of a tailspin. But six years after the duo split for good, reissues have introduced Rap & Polo's hardcore landmarks to a whole new audience. Listening to "Streets Of New York", you feel kinda like one of those white guys in the background. Keep quiet, and you won't get hurt. . .

LAURYN HILL

Doo Wap (That Thing)

(THE MISEDUCATION OF LAURYN HILL, SONY 2000)

"It's silly when girls sell their souls because it's in"

THE FUGEES

Boof Bap

(BLUNTED ON REALITY, SONY 1994)

**"I'll love your theory like the chi-chi-woo-woo-boogie-man
You say I'm balanced but you're Silence of the Lambs"**

OK, a tale of two records. One a tantalizing glimpse of a new talent with new things to say and new ways of saying them, tapping into the rich racial lineage that gave birth to much old-skool hip hop whilst combining it with a political sense that was able to take in the experiences not just of rap's normal constituency but the other racial minorities (Asian, Haitian, Cuban) who were starting to see rap as their own new language of resistance in the early nineties. Loved in hip hop circles, ignored by the rest of the world. The other album a self-indulgent, funkless suite of navel-gazing tedium augmented with beats so polite they could slip easily around the coffee tables of a whole generation of rap-hating middle-aged white liberals. Loved by everyone, critics, audience, media and pop historians alike. For most of the world *The Miseducation Of Lauryn Hill* was the hip hop album of the 90s it was OK to

like. For hip hop fans it was proof of the nauseatingly patronizing way the mainstream pop culture would think it understood where hip hop's cutting edge was, even whilst they were merely getting nearer to the point where hip hop lost it's point, started to suckle on a bloated industry teat that could only lead to creative death and the mediocrity that mass appeal requires.

We'd been used to pop hip hop of course. Hammer and Vanilla and the myriad chancers who used a faint understanding of hip hop in the late eighties and early nineties to enact bankraids on the pop marketplace: what the catastrophic deterioration of Lauryn Hill's talent proved was that no hip hop could emerge from its interface with the industry without somehow compromising itself, alienating itself from the hip hop audience. Lauryn Hill's contributions to the Fugees brilliant debut album were some of that record's highlights – here was a female MC not just intent on matching men rhyme-for-flow but seemingly engrossed in her own variety of personas, as self-intrigued as every great rapper should be but possessed of a compassion and empathy in her storytelling that earmarked her as a new Nina Simone, someone able to inhabit many heads at the same time, expressing the full complexity and contradiction of her place in space. By the time Lauryn Hill had gone through the industry mangler (as initiated by the gruesome success of The Fugees' totally overrated *The Score* follow-up, boosted by the karaoke-hideousness of "Killing Me Softly") and "Doo Wap" was officially consecrated as the hip hop single it was OK to listen to in 2000, we knew that we could never believe the mainstream media again about the music we loved. "Doo Wap" was an average song, blazed to international acclaim by the kind of people who would be surreptitiously giving donations to the PMRC if they could: the fact that such a transparently overstretched talent as Hill's was getting hailed as hip hop's second coming showed the sham results of letting non-believers dip their toes in rap's dirty water.

**Big talent, dwindling
returns: Lauryn Hill.**

LL COOL J

I Can't Live Without My Radio

(RADIO, DEF JAM, 1987)

"Wearin' light blue Pumas, a whole lotta gold/And jams like these keep me in control. . . "

Those of you reading this alphabetically might be wondering about the leap we just made. Straight from Lauryn Hill to Cool J? What about Kool Moe Dee? How can you leave Moe Dee out and include Cool J when one of the first and most long-running beefs in hip hop was between the Kool one and the Cool one? Remember Moe Dee's cover for *How Ya Like Me Now* – a red Kangol hat (Cool J's trademark) being crushed by the wheels of a jeep (subtle yet effective)? Well, I've already admitted that what this book has to leave out (don't even get me started on Camp Lo, Chino XL, Kwest The Madd Ladd, Boogiemonsters, Real Live, New Kingdom etc etc) is gonna upset people (including me), but sometimes you have to admit that in rap rivalry there is a winner. Cool J wins out not just cos his career outlasted his many nay-sayers but because "'Radio" is still a great record, still pumps your fists and your veins with the same, adrenalized, teenage aggression it always did. Find me a Moe Dee track that still has that effect and I'll be willing to reconsider.

In fact, the painful thing with Cool J is that for an artist barely listened to any more (too ancient to be a real, lasting influence, too uncool to be an old-skool hero) he made too many great tracks that could've been included here. "Jack The Ripper", "Go Cut Creator Go", "I'm Bad" – even after his supposed falling off (after *Bigger And Deffer*), he was still giving up genius like "Eat Em Up L Chill", "Goin' Back To Cali" and "Crossroads".

Part of what's made Cool J such an indefatigable talent is his sheer, irrepressible likeability. Even as he was making the brashest boasts, indulging in the most gruesome self-aggrandizement, he did it with a look, a cheek, a grin that suggested he was finding the whole shebang of being a rap superstar as ridiculous as you were, a wonderfully self-aware note of irony that informed all his work. It came from the fact that Cool J grew up in the business, found his first fame at the age of 16.

Hollis hip-hop hero
Uncle LL Cool J.

Born James Todd Smith in Queens, Cool J started rapping at age nine, after his grandfather bought him his first DJ equipment. By thetime he was 13, he was processing his first demos and sending them out to every single record company he could find.

The first to respond to his mail-outs was Rick Rubin at Def Jam, then a senior at NYU (alongside fellow-alumni Russell Simmons), who signed him to the fledgling label in 1984. Def Jam's first-ever release was the twelve of "I Need A Beat", which was also Cool J's recording debut. The single sold 100,000 copies, making the label's name overnight and the 17-year-old Cool J's future standing with the same speed. *Radio*, the album that followed after Cool J had dropped out of high-school, was a major hit and something of a first for hip hop: here was an album in which the tracks seemed not to emerge from hours of material, music that didn't seem chopped down from rambling freestyles and party sets.

Tracks like "I Can't Live Without My Radio" were revelatory because they seemed to be crafted as pop tracks, that length for a reason rather than artificially chopped off at the heels when the producer got bored, while the things Cool J rapped about were miles away from the grown-up, authoritarian nature of rap until then, and way more like the testimony of a real B-boy. This wasn't just music that appealed to rap fans, it was music about being a rap fan, and that made a link of fidelity between J and his audience that it took a decade to truly desecrate.

Cool J was featured heavily in the *Krush Groove* film (as was *Radio*) and in the wake of that movie's success, J was asked to embark on a 50-city US tour alongside Fat Boys, Whodini, Grandmaster Flash and Run DMC. DMC were crucial to Cool J's ensuing development. What had clearly occurred by the time *Bigger And Deffer* came out was J's ability to drop rhymes that spoke of the B-boy life we were all living, while using beats with the same control, care and authority that DMC had bought to hip hop (like DMC, Cool J would let Rick Rubin run riot on *Radio*, dropping as much rock guitar as he could manage to get into the swirl).

"I Can't Live Without My Radio" was the track that made Cool J a hip hop hero and set him on an upward spiral. The wickedly torsioned turns that spiral took through gig violence, pop hits, hip hop rejection, meeting presidents and making sit-coms and movies aren't even hinted at, and that's it's innocent charm. The sound of young America in 1985 didn't get much hotter than this.

LUDACRIS

What's Your Fantasy

(BACK FOR THE FIRST TIME, DEF JAM, 2000)

"I wanna do in the canopy/I wanna do it where your girl gon see and get mad at me. . . "

JUVENILE

Ha

(400 DEGREEZ, CASH MONEY/UNIVERSAL, 1998)

"I'm the one/Stick a fork in that nigga cause he's done. . . "

Tutored in positivity, knowledge and the universally redemptive power of communication and honesty – that's what you feel you ought to be as a B-boy, as a fan of hip hop, this artform that's changed and changes your life. You feel that even though hip hop documents some of the worse impulses in a human heart (and/or groin), it gives you an insightful knowledge, an essential, discursive distance that enables you to see through such base motives and come to your own conclusions, certainly in respect to how you feel within the music and where you think you belong within its moral framework (sometimes as willing fellow-combatant, sometimes as conscientious objector).

But, occasionally, hip hop doesn't impress you with its mind. It just fucks with your head and before you know it, you're saddled to a beat and a loop you know you'll never forget – and you're enjoying ideas you know for a fact are normally morally repugnant to you. It was difficult in the heat and hurry of the Dirty South hip hop explosion of the late nineties (represented here by these two monsters), to know where you stood in relation to this music, whether you should be an outraged observer or admit your pretensions towards hip hop enlightenment had to be abandoned, and simply get in on this ugly ruckus. Clearly morally bankrupt, barely educational in terms of letting you into a mindset not your own, purely the goading encouragement of all the worst thoughts that come to a person unfortunate enough to have a dick – this was macho music, totally sexist music, totally hopeless music, as suspicious of anyone holding out hopes of redemption as it was possible to be. As a listener, you felt trapped between surrendering to the undeniable drive of the music and throwing your elbows out to stop the sickness.

Maybe it was the fact that Dirty South rap music always had to overcome hurdles to get heard; maybe that explained its vulgar appetite for attention.

Ludacris: Rappers shouldn't even look like they're thinking about dancing, exhibit one.

Less moneyed-up than their coastal cousins, impresarios like Cash Money's Williams brothers and Master P put out shoddily packaged, repetitively themed LPs with all the high-minded appeal of amateur pornography knowing that, musically, they were on to something special. Within the albums, behind the lurid covers, amazing things were occurring.

Juveline's "Ha" was one of the first tunes that seemed totally dominated by its beat, a maddening, thug-futurist skronk of bass'n'bleeps'n'technoid noise that sounded like nothing else in rap. Pretty soon the "hot" beats were what was dominating hip hop, the MC's role reduced from that of a poetic visionary to that of he who must seek the "hottest" producers to frame his lack of lyrical depth. "Ha" was the track that took Cash Money Records into the big league, way outselling everything else on the fledgling label and focusing industry attention on the Dirty South for the first time in hip hop history – attention that Ludacris was to benefit from. The Atlanta-based rapper went from local sensation to household name after Def Jam's A&R man, Scarface, signed him to its Def Jam South subsidiary in 2000.

In addition to connecting him with super-producers like Timbaland, The Neptunes and Organized Noize, Def Jam gave Ludacris a remarkable marketing push. He thus, quickly, became one of the rap industry's most in-demand rappers, guesting on hits for everyone from Missy Elliott ("One Minute Man") to Jermaine Dupri ("Welcome to Atlanta") when he wasn't dominating the urban market with his own hits, notably "What's Your Fantasy".

Atlanta was the south's rap Mecca in the mid-nineties, and Ludacris moved from being a radio jock to working with Timbaland before "What's Your Fantasy" propelled him to national prominence. An explicit duet about sexual fantasies from both the male and female perspective, "What's Your Fantasy" was at least as musically astonishing as anything Juvenile gave us, a frighteningly cold song about sex that reconvened the battle of the sexes as a robotic battle and orgy. It was perhaps the most explicitly techno-informed hip hop we'd heard since Bambaataa's "Planet Rock", or the Ultramags, but run alongside a whole new way with beats and drum patterns that owed much more to drum'n'bass and Aphex Twin than to old-skool funk. Rap's current, dwindling hot-beat returns can be traced back to these two bombs. Further than that, rap could no longer simply be considered a turf war between the two coasts. The south did rise again.

The South's finest, Ludacris goes nowhere without his rhyme skulls.

Live At The Barbeque

(BREAKING ATOMS, WILD PITCH, 1990)

"Why's my name the Large Professor?/Cause I milked your cow in other words I hit your heffer. . . "

Main Source are one of the hidden gems of hip hop history, a band who only really came together on one album and then went their separate ways, a band who created a classic so beloved by hip hop fans who bought it that securing yourself a copy now takes some effort. Like a lot of releases on Wild Pitch by artists including OC, The Coup and Lord Finesse, people won't part with *Breaking Atoms*, won't lend it to you, seem almost reticent to make a tape of such a holy document. My copy is scratched to buggery but still gets played with great fondness.

Breaking Atoms works because, like so much that came in its wake, it determinedly creates a sumptuously funky music from sources no one could trace. Ignoring the P-Funk and James Brown samples the rest of rap was busy running dry, MS's production dream team of the Large Professor, DJ K-Cut and Sir Scratch culled their collages from records you couldn't imagine and made one of the most effective, smoked-out, sampladelic masterpieces that rap had ever produced.

Large Professor's incredibly clever wordplay (check out the baseball-themed, police-brutality banger, "Just A Friendly Game Of Baseball", and the heartbreakingly dysfunctional "Looking At The Front Door") set a new standard in terms of the wit and restraint rappers could bring to difficult subjects. Only now can we look back and see how much else was going on, how Large Professor and K would go on to mould so much future hip hop, tutoring DJ Premier on how to use the SP1200, giving Akinyele and Nas their debut cameos on the stunning "Live At The Barbeque". After *Breaking Atoms*, the Professor would go on to make classics with Eric B & Rakim, Mobb Deep, Nas and Pete Rock, but nothing touches the work he accomplished with Main Source.

The first rolling-out of a hip hop legend.

MANTRONIX
Fresh Is The Word

(12", SLEEPING BAG, 1985)

Without Mantronix, one wonders if hip hop production would have ever developed beyond the turntable, ever found the bristling, futurist edge that pushes it beyond the ones and twos and into genuine, sonic invention of new sounds. Without Mantronix, it would have been possible to see to see hip hop rapidly dying as it ran out of obvious samples to hijack. Flash's experimentalism with decks was a high point but a dead-end in terms of hip hop's future. Unless hip hop was willing to embrace production possibilities that had nothing to do with the block parties of its birth, those block parties would've been exactly where it stayed.

Hip hop's relationship with technology was always founded on what was affordable to its practitioners: in the late seventies and early eighties, that was decks and very little else. Mantronix, overseen and controlled by Kurtis Mantronik, were crucial, not just because he expanded the variety and forms of hip hop's creative tools but because he always came at technology with a thoroughly old-skool, hip hop attitude. You never got the feeling with Mantronik that he was trying to improve hip hop from without; rather, he was abusing technology with a hip hop attitude and a willful amateurism that allowed him to experiment without fear of incorrectness and without concern for the spods and science-club geeks who'd had control over pop technology for so long. Instruction manuals weren't just bunk to Kurtis, they were accursed texts of confinement and anti-creativity. Only when those manuals were ignored and contradicted could hip hop find a use for the technology that was coming its way. Mantronix were crucial in letting rap know it had nothing to fear from the future.

Born Kurtis Khaleel in Jamaica, Mantronik and family moved to Canada and then New York. By the late seventies, he was DJing around the city, and he met MC Tee (born Tooure Embden) while working behind the decks at Manhattan's Downtown Records. The duo assembled a demo tape and gave it to William Socolov, president of Sleeping Bag Records. "Fresh Is The Word" tore up New York in 1985. It still sounds fearlessly futurist now, a mad, mechanoid mash-up of disco, funk, electro and pure hip hop that led to a welter of production jobs for Kurtis. He signed EPMD to Sleeping Bag, produced KRS-One's first credit ("Success Is The Word" by 12.41), and desk-jockeyed tracks by Tricky Tee, Just Ice and T La Rock. Mantronix would eventually move on from rap to techno and dance, but the seed had been sown by "Fresh Is The Word" and the *Music Madness* album. Hip hop's inferiority complex to the rest of music had finally been completely eroded.

White Lines (Don't Do It)

(12", SUGAR HILL, 1983)

"Orang dang diggedy dang di-dang/Orang dang diggedy dang di-dang. . ."

I remember it quite distinctly. Being driven to school in a Hillman Imp. 1983. I had just turned 12. Radio blaring, typical morning show bollocks. None of which mattered to me. Pop music just seemed shit. All music seemed shit in 1983, made by weird grown-ups who weren't from the same planet as you. So that morning's DJ yatter and pop wank washed over me like every other morning. Pulled up to a red light. I still remember the junction. The DJ says he's gonna play some "rapping" music. A moment's silence.

And then my life began. "White Lines" was the first hip hop track I ever loved, the first moment of my existence. When its harmonies kicked in, I felt like I'd never felt before – i.e., I felt something. When a bassline so instantly hot-wired into your memory came booming out of our shitty, car tranny, I think I felt my first sexual stirrings. I shifted in the back seat of the Imp, wondering if that engine in the boot was causing that throbbing, or something scarily elsewhere. When this voice, this impossibly supacool, booming voice that I'd

later discover belonged to Grandmaster Melle Mel said, "bass", I knew I'd stumbled across a new way of talking and walking and living. It changed what I spent my money on, the clothes I wore, the films I watched, the books I read, the drugs I'd take, the words I'd say.

The next week, I went into Woolworths and bought "White Lines" on 12". It was the first record I ever bought. Friends who'd taped it off the radio were impressed that I'd already learnt every line, could rap along word for word. Perhaps it was best that I didn't know what in God's name the track was about. Dimly aware it was something to do with drugs, I was too young to realize that the guy intoning this gospel was a junkie himself, would admit in the future that when he was in the studio in 1982 laying down the vocal track, the "only thing I was thinking about in that studio was listening to the record, joking and getting high". Perhaps it was best not to know too much about your heroes back then, to keep them at far more of a distance than the mere three thousand miles between New York City and Coventry. Whoever was making this "rap" music sounded incredibly cool, incredibly clever, had a way with words that was totally absorbing, a way of making poetry come so fast you didn't have time to acknowledge each amazing rhyme. And the music didn't sound like other music at the time: there was no whiney thinness here, no pompous, trebly prettiness. This was big-bottomed music, music that hit you in the guts and the ass with a primitive yet brilliantly arranged thump that was seemingly created for simpletons like you.

GRANDMASTER FLASH & MELLE MEL

Melle Mel wrote many of the legendary raps featured on Grandmaster Flash & The Furious Five tracks. When the huge success of "The Message" fractured the group (Flash and Mel weren't happy about sharing composer credits with Sylvia Robinson, wife of Sugar Hill domo Joe Robinson), a court battle allowed Mel to add the soubriquet "Grandmaster" and Sugar Hill to release "White Lines". The key to the track is its ambiguity, a supposedly anti-drugs declaration that makes taking drugs sound utterly cool and whose music perfectly replicates the neon-hot breeze of cocaine. Mel added the "Don't Do It" parenthesis when one of his friends, a dealer, died a few weeks before its release. He'd have one more good year in him (in '84, he guested on Chaka Kahn's international smash, "I Feel For You", one of the first exposures rap received in the mainstream, and he appeared in the movie *Beat Street*), but "White Lines" remains Mel's crowning moment in pop history. For quite a few B-boys, it was the moment we first got involved in this carnage. We salute you.

MISSY ELLIOTT

Get Ur Freak On

(MISS E. . . SO ADDICTIVE, ELEKTRA/ASYLUM, 2001)

**"WHO'S THAT BIIIITCH? People you don't know?
Me and Timbaland been hot since twenty years ago. . . "**

One of only two women in this book. See it as an indictment of hip hop and not me. While Nefertiti, Eve, Lil' Kim, Bahamadia, Erykah Badu, Foxy Brown and plenty of others have made great records, Missy is the first female hip hop artist who seems genuinely to be changing attitudes within the rap community towards women in the industry. If rap's next stage is to accept that anyone who wants to use its magic to express themselves should be able to do so (and it clearly is), then Missy can be seen as an avatar for the next century of hip hop. She's got there not through hostile self-definition but because you love her. That's all you can do. She makes nothing else an option.

She knows that the complexities of the image she presents in her award-hoovering videos are purely pretend, glorious, fantastical, pixilated play, intending to fuck with convention and reveal her own schizophrenic desires. Still, they only hint at the true, deeper, psychological complication that bubbles within, something that can only find a real voice in sound waves and beats. Missy Elliot has had to be so damn busy being a hip hop star since her explosion on to the scene with *Supa Dupa Fly* in 1997 but, at heart, she's a muso in the strictest sense, a sonically obsessed studio freak with the passionate commitment to innovation of a Delia Derbyshire and the pop sensibility of any kid who grew up in headphones and bedrooms, captivated by plastic. Ask her about her most surreal moment and it's like the posters climbed off the wall and into her life and she still can't get her head around it.

"The most surreal moment of my career? I could name so many. When I got my first phone call from Janet. My first phone call from Whitney. My first phone call from Mariah. The first time I spoke to Madonna. Getting a call from Michael Jackson. In my mind, I was like, 'I think people need to stop playing with my phone. I'm going to have to get my number changed.' I'm still in groupie mode. Madonna was somebody I watched on TV, and I put on all those belts and gloves and started singing 'Like a Virgin' in my room. You couldn't tell me I wasn't the black Madonna. So, to get those phone calls, I never adjusted to that. Each one was like, 'Wow!'"

If she came into rap like a gleeful whirlwind, it's still blowing, power undimmed or expended half a decade on. Five smash-hit albums already before 2003, at which point any self-respecting head (for that is what she truly is) would take a few years to recover, get strung-out, lazy, rest on laurels that are starting to rot. The thing is with Missy, she just will not stop. The cool thing about Missy is that she hasn't got that fatal, blasé attitude about pop – "I'm an insider." She still talks like an outsider looking in, like the rest of us, like a fan.

An only child born in small-town Portsmouth, Virginia, in 1971, she grew up in a household where her father was either ignoring her or beating the shit out of her mum. Retreating into her imagination, the young Melissa Elliott used to sing and perform imaginary gigs in her bedroom to an audience of dolls. To her mute, plastic posse she perfected her rhyme skills, her voice, her dance moves. Hooking up with a girl group, Sista, and signing to Jodeci member Devante Swing's Swing Mob Records, Missy and pal Tim "Timbaland" Mosley set about writing songs for Jodeci's *Diary Of A Mad Band* album.

Sista fell apart, the label folded, and Missy and Timba started working for Aaliyah – legendary production jobs ("One In A Million" and "If Your Girl Only Knew") that put Missy in popular demand as a producer. It wasn't enough. She wanted the mic, she wanted the stage, and she wanted to make her own music. But she was forced to settle for guest-rapping wherever she could as one label after another rebuffed her because her image didn't fit. Her non-anorexic size and freewheeling lyrical talent, it was felt, would be too much for the audience to handle.

Eventually, she signed to Elektra in '96 for the *Supa Dupa Fly* album, replete with single "The Rain", which vigorously answered the many other industry doubters. Yet, her earlier, harsh experiences have seemingly informed Missy's career ever since: they definitely account for her never-half-assed celebration of populist futurism and her total resistance to the patriarchal domination of hip hop.

It's her startlingly normal attitude, the self-deprecation and awareness behind the transformations she stages, that make Missy an inspiration for anyone, male or female, wanting to break out of that bedroom and into the spotlight.

But perhaps what's most inspirational about Missy Elliott isn't the way she stands in such glorious isolation from the machinations of the biz. It's the way she's played the music business so adeptly while retaining her doubt, her crucial knowledge of the mangler that keeps her from getting sucked in and ultimately crushed.

For every ad campaign and line in lipsticks, there are profits ploughed into the domestic-violence charity Break The Cycle, a 100,000 square-foot Virginian home for her mum, and her own production/management company, The Gold Mind. She's a woman with power who knows the still-concrete limits and ceilings thrown around that power, a serious-as-hell musician who knows the strength of a single the world falls in love with. That Missy single *par excellence* is "Get Ur Freak On" – Timba and his main imaginative partner at the absolute top of their form. In the future, this'll be called seminal. From a woman. No shit.

MOBB DEEP

Survival Of The Fittest

(THE INFAMOUS, RCA, 1995)

"Lord forgive me the Hennessy got me not knowin' how to act/I'm fallin' and I can't turn back. . . "

Prior to *The Infamous*, one of the greatest, hardcore hip hop albums of all time, Mobb Deep were only really of interest to hip hop heads because of their collaborators. Straight outta Queensbridge, New York, an area that also gave us Marley Marl and Nas, Havoc and Prodigy – who made up Mobb Deep – recorded their debut LP, *Juvenile Hell*, as teenagers, with DJ Premier and Large Professor at the controls. Havoc also guested on the awesome Black Moon's "U Da Man". But *The Infamous* was something else.

Self-produced bar a few, final mix-downs by the Abstract (Q-Tip's producer pseudonym), *The Infamous* was pretty much the perfect combination of dead-on, representin' lyrics and music that hit on a sublime mix of scary, scratchy, stereo-separated samples and punishing, icy beats. Like Nas and Wu-Tang (both of whom guested), Mobb's lyrics were simultaneously locked in on their own world and murderously intent on understanding a wider, even grimmer reality wherein the realization that you were mortal both overpowered and deeply depressed you. As a result, certain words and themes kept recurring throughout *The Infamous* almost as totems of safety, all they could be sure of.

"Survival Of the Fittest" sums up MD's brutal grace and pitiless analysis. It was simply one of the most chilling, atmospheric hip hop tracks we'd heard since the heyday of Eric B. Taking what sounds like a Rachmaninoff piano crystal (OK, could've been Erik Satie, could be Thelonius Monk – whatever, it was a sample as perfect and startling as Jeru The Damaja's "Come Clean" or Nas's "N.Y. State Of Mind") and looping it with blunted horns and an old-skool beat, MD span out a track that trip-hoppers would try, and fail, to emulate for the rest of the nineties.

Mobb Deep's production style became a touchstone, their sense of haunting melody and hard-hitting beats perfectly suiting the bleak nature of the duo's rhymes. And in an era when Jay-Z was making *Reasonable Doubt* and Nas was making *Illmatic*, Mobb Deep were the kings, creating a style of beat-making and a lyrical connection with real street terrors that no one else could match. Greater fame, and infamy, would come MD's way but "Survival Of The Fittest" remains one of nineties hip hop's most enduringly shocking, eternally beautiful, moments.

N.Y. State Of Mind

(ILLMATIC, COLUMBIA, 1994)

"Inhale deep like the words of my breath/I never sleep, cause sleep is the cousin of death. . . "

Whether by accident, happy coincidence or design, the sleeve to Nas's first album was crucial in implanting the spectral and mysterious hold he had over us in 1994. A shot of a kid, possibly Nas himself, not a pretty, album-cover kid but a real kid, with the project housing blocks of Queensbridge superimposed across his face. Not a lot to it, but it looked as if those blocks were the kid's own internal geography, as if his environment had come to inhabit him as much as he disappeared into his environment. For a debut album not to announce its arrival in a riot of close-ups and gold and bad streetwear was novel in itself; for a sleeve to hint so quietly and subtly at the depth of thought within was a blessed relief. Further than that, it suggested something downright heretical: that the artist you would hear on the record wasn't just in a purely utilitarian relationship to the streets on which he lived, he was also just as able to dream of those streets, to fantasize within those streets and be spun out into a mental fog as well as a sudden clarity by those streets. And if those hints were enough to draw you in, then "N.Y. State Of Mind" kept you there. A more concrete yet somehow abstract moment doesn't exist in nineties rap music.

Born Nasir Jones, son of jazz musician Olu Dara, Nas dropped out of school in the eighth grade, trading classrooms for the streets of the rough, Queensbridge projects, long-fabled as the former stomping ground of Marley Marl and his Juice Crew, immortalized in "The Bridge". Entrusted with his own education, Jones immersed himself in both high literature and real life, both of which would inform his later work. His crush of finely honed wordplay and street-smart imagery would come to its first fruition in 1991 when he connected with Main Source to drop an unforgettable stanza on "Live at the Barbeque" that earned him instant respect among the east-coast rap scene. Not long afterward, MC Serch of 3rd Bass approached Nas about contributing a track to the *Zebrahead* soundtrack. Nas submitted "Halftime", and the now-classic track so stunned Serch that he made it the soundtrack's lead-off track.

Columbia signed Nas to a major-label contract. DJ Premier, Large Professor and Pete Rock lined up to work with him. And *Illmatic* was created. Absolutely free of the pop concessions that would characterize and catastrophically undermine his later work (for hip hop heads if not for sales), Illmatic stands as one of the all-time-great, hip hop debuts and "N.Y. State Of Mind" one of the greatest album lead-off tracks ever. A shuffling maze of piano and drone with a beat that perfectly replicated a stumbling voyage around hyper-tense streets, its lyrics and music seemed to put the intimate psychogeography of Nas' stomping ground into the head of the listener. This wasn't cultural tourism, it was a breakneck introduction not just to Nas' environment but also to the mental impact that that environment had made. It put everyone right inside Jones' supra-aware consciousness, letting you feel both the extreme intelligence yet very human doubt that dwelled there. After Biggie died and east-coast DJs started competing for the vacant throne of New York hip hop, Nas abandoned his journey of self-discovery in favour of shameless popularity-chasing and needless beefs with Jay-Z. "N.Y. State Of Mind" captures him at that sublime moment when his talent was focused on the truth and not lost in the smoke and mirrors of status.

NAUGHTY BY NATURE

O.P.P.

(12", TOMMY BOY, 1990)

"How many brothers out there know just what I'm getting' at/Who thinks its wrong cos I'm splittin and co-hittin at. . . "

You down with OPP?

OK, I split the world into three camps. The ones who are scratching their heads. The ones who immediately bellow back, "Yeah!! You know me!!" And the ones who are faintly embarrassed, trying not to laugh out loud behind their smugness, their smirks. Yeah, yeah, quit your snickering at the back – you should've seen some of the pop hip hop tracks I didn't include. Salutary lessons as they may be in the transitory nature of fame, I don't consider MC Hammer's "U Can't Touch This" or Vanilla Ice's "Ice Ice Baby" as worthy of inclusion in a book about hip hop, because they weren't really hip hop. They were pop shit that borrowed from hip hop. just as legions of bad hip house/techno hop acts will always do.

Frankly, there's more importance in ESG (who sold very few records) than MC Hammer (biggest-selling rap artist of the late-eighties) for the purposes of this volume, so why include Naughty By Nature?

Well, at this point I have to put down my pen, throw an arm around your shoulders, down about twenty beers and throw on "O.P.P." at top volume. Still frowning? Expression of a fool.

Everyone was down with "O.P.P." in the early nineties. (Indeed, who didn't "Hip Hop Hooray" to its follow-up smash the following year?) If you've never been in a club and put your hands in the air and waved 'em like you just don't care to "O.P.P." I reckon you're a hermit or a liar or both. A transgenerational hip hop phenomenon, with young and old alike chanting along to the bumptious "O.P.P." (little knowing they were endorsing the safari-like hunt of "Other People's Pussy"), it gave hip hop a much-needed feel of unity in the early nineties, and one of the all-time, classic, party tunes of all time. You pretty much know the lyrics to most NBN hits off by heart, mainly cos it takes about one minute to learn them. But that's what kept them at the top of their game for so long. They've sold four million copies of their albums combined, and the infectious run of singles they gave us in the early nineties ("O.P.P.", "Uptown Anthem", "Ghetto Bastard", "Jamboree", "Feel Me Flow" and "Hip Hop Hooray") always managed just enough ruggedness to keep the heads churlishly shaking a tail feather (but not smiling) while everyone else could just get down. Got a problem with that? Go and stand in the corner. You're forgetting where and why hip hop was born. To make people dance. Never forget it.

NBN's short-lived flirtation with the stagecraft of Howard Jones was a trying period for the band.

N.E.R.D.

Lapdance

(IN SEARCH OF, VIRGIN, 2002)

"Cause this society, that makes a nigga wanna kill!/I'm just straight ill! Ridin' my motorcycle down the streets. . . "

"Got My Money" (Ol' Dirty Bastard), "Shake Ya Ass" (Mystikal), "I Just Wanna Love U (Give It To Me)" (Jay-Z), "Pass The Courvoisier (Busta Rhymes featuring P Diddy and Pharrell Williams)", "Hot In Herre" (Nelly), "Frontin'" (Pharrell Williams featuring Jay-Z), "Excuse Me Miss" (Jay-Z featuring Pharrell Williams), "When The Last Time (Clipse featuring Kelis and Pharrell Williams)" – the list of hits Pharrell Williams and Chad Hugo have been responsible for in millennial hip hop is quite staggering, especially when you consider just how inventive those hits have been, just what a bold, new and total sonic aesthetic The Neptunes have forced into rap, pulled pop into, turned the world on to. Unheralded on their emergence from sleepy Virginia Beach, their ascendancy has been as complete as it has been meteoric, and, like all the best genii, their brilliance lies in their simplicity. What The Neptunes realized couldn't have been realized before, wouldn't have sounded as naturally right for the times before now – yet beneath its superficial complexity lies some fairly straightforward magic. The Neptunes are knowledgeable hip hop heads who've simply reversed the roles of a normal production for the genre.

Where before, hip hop's sound relied on a steady beat, slower than the rap that would go on top of it so that the music couched the words, The Neptunes have done the opposite. The words punctuate the music, holding its bones together with something muscular, steadily intoning phrases behind the rhythmic, syncopated busyness of the drum patterns and loops. Because the oddity of the format is so gripping, the seemingly effortless, identikit nature of Neptunes productions is less a hindrance than a help, so long as the details of the mix are kept fresh with new variants.

But when Chad and Pharrell announced they were beginning their own rap/rock group, N.E.R.D., the psychedelic, labyrinthine textures and timbres of their debut album, *In Search Of*, managed to exceed all expectations. Here was music that suggested way more than mere studio-smarts at work; here was music with soul, feeling, a uniquely cloistered, intense and intimate vibe they haven't yet been able to achieve with their more obviously outré, farmed-out productions. "Lapdance", the lead-off single, cooked up a tangible, fuzzed-up heat even more infectious than their work for Jay.

If The Neptunes' sonic sorcery, its returns now dwindling, is to yield any future dividend, then their capability for shade and deep focus is surely what needs to be brought back into their beautifully strobed universe. Noughties hip hop without peer.

THE NOTORIOUS B.I.G.

Big Poppa

(READY TO DIE, BAD BOY, 1994)

"A T-bone steak, cheese eggs and Welch's grape/Conversate for a few, cause in a few, we gon' do. . ."

2PAC
California Love

(ALL EYEZ ON ME, DEATH ROW, 2001)

"Out on bail fresh out of jail, California dreamin'/Soon as I step on the scene, I'm hearin hoochies screamin'. . ."

It may seem a tad obvious to include these two together. Throughout their lives, their stories and mythologies were intertwined to such an extent that their deaths in close proximity seemed almost too fictionally perfect, too brutal a twist in the tale to be believable. Ever since, 2Pac and Biggie have been the twin-towering martyrs of hip hop – so much so that any doubting of their lasting legacy and influence is tantamount to pulling a hip hop 9/11.

But the reason I've put them together isn't just to tie up the strands of an ugly story that symbolizes all that was ugliest about nineties hip hop, in particular the coastal turf wars that both bored and bewildered us into a dazed, numb, fatal acceptance of these two rappers' untimely and violent passing. The reason I've put them together is because I think they were equally bad rappers, equally overrated talents and equally deserving of reappraisal. Everybody loves you when you're dead. But just as John Lennon's assassination, Kurt Cobain's suicide and Princess Diana's car crash shouldn't stop us calling a hippie a hippie, a junkie a junkie and a parasitical clotheshorse a parasitical clotheshorse, so Biggie and Tupac's admittedly tragic

**Self-confessed mummy's boy,
The Notorious B.I.G.**

ends shouldn't stop any B-boy from calling 'em out for who they were: thoroughly mediocre talents, possibly bought down by forces they set in motion but couldn't control, possibly the unfortunate victims of corrupt cops and self-appointed criminal avengers. Definitely bad rappers, both, and that's what concerns us here.

What galls the most about both MCs' posthumous canonization is that their lives are now misrepresented as lessons in the dangers of the hip hop lifestyle and mindset, often by precisely the people who'd seek to glamorize that supposed lifestyle, to prop up the hip hop industry as it rumbles on with the same old war stories, the same need for tabloid fuel. Secretly, in the heart of everyone who mourned them so extravagantly, was the thought – it had to be this way, it's the ending to the potboiler that we wanted. It does both hip hop, and Biggie and Tupac, a great disservice to review their lives in such dumbly, karmic fashion.

Yet it's always easier than apprehending the genuine, unredemptive waste of life to feel secure in the knowledge that the "hip- hop lifestyle" (for these dolts, "the criminal lifestyle") should get the blame.

But, hold on a minute. Was 2Pac or Biggie leading a lifestyle that had anything to do with what they rapped about? Wasn't 2Pac a sensitive soul trapped in an increasingly outdated persona, trying to break out of that persona as he realised how untenably inauthentic it was? Wasn't Biggie a big, soft, momma's boy at heart, a middle-class dealer in package-trip, ghetto chicanery who'd only pass up mom's apple pie for an opportunity to sell crack to those poorer and less fortunate than himself?

2Pac's journey from second-string rapper and dancer for Digital Underground to navel-gazing, soft-centred, tough-guy superstar had way more to do with his brilliant ability as an actor than as an MC. The outlaw mythology he surrounded and steeped himself in was no reason for him to die. And his death turned 2Pac's real crimes (fights that ended up killing six-year-old bystanders, sexual assault) into forgivable, juicy detail, life scars that made those dreamboat eyes more poignant. Much of the intrigue that followed Shakur's death (was he trying to leave Death Row, was it Biggie retaliating for Pac's jibes about his wife, was it payback for the shooting of Randy Walker, was it the fight in the Casino?) still bubbles on – all of it blinding people to the fact that the vast bulk of Pac's recorded work (bar "California Love", which couldn't fail with its Dre production and Roger Troutman's vocoder cameo) is monumentally dull, tediously produced, snoozeworthy G-Funk that only someone as disinterested in music as Suge Knight would put his money behind. The fact it was a sound investment, the fact that the coffin-chasing hordes have ensured Knight's made mucho dinero from Pac's death, is irrelevant. 2Pac made mainly bad hip hop.

Similarly, I find it difficult to see that when Biggie joined Sean "Puffy" Combs in moving from Uptown to form Bad Boy, it was as an epochal moment in hip hop history, mainly because it resulted in such middling music. Ready To Die is far from the classic of its romantic reputation. True, Biggie possessed way more natural MC talent than 2Pac, but the patchiness of his recorded output (killer tracks like "Big Poppa" next to unforgivably maddening dross) stops him from being recalled by me with any real fondness. He was a larger-than-life figure allowed to get away with too much nonchalant, lazy averageness by the dullards who indulged and surrounded him.

As with Tupac, listening to any of Biggie's music convinces you that the bullets that killed them both are the only things ensuring their immortality right now, 'cos the joints they threw down while they were still breathing sure as fuck don't ensure that. And the distractive sideshow that the EC/WC beefs threw up (now replaced by the equally dull, internecine bitching going on between Nas and Jay-Z and Ja Rule and Eminem and blahblahblah) surely can't keep us believers in the fiction of this mournful sycophancy any more. Together in life, in death, in future irrelevance.

Police

(LIVE, SONY 2000)

"Mais cette notion d'humanisme n'existe plus quand ils passent l'uniforme"

NTM's "Police" was the record that bought native hip hop to the awareness of mainstream European culture – it, together with the film *Le Haine*, were instrumental in boldly stating that hip hop had found it's way into our lives yet was being bent by us into shapes that fitted THIS life, these streets, this corner of the planet. Performing at an anti-racism Bastille Day concert, the two rappers Kool Shen and Joey Starr of NTM encouraged the audience to shout "nique la police" in the direction of security: found guilty by a court of "orally abusing" the security forces, NTM were sentenced to six months in prison, fined 50,000 francs, and disbanded for six months. On appeal, NTM's ban from "professional activity" was reduced to two months, but "l'affaire NTM" and further anti-state rhymes provoked a political and cultural backlash. Le Pen's xenophobic National Front denounced rap as "a dangerous art which originated in Algiers" and warned that graffiti appearing on banlieues walls was threatening French civilization. The popularity of hip hop is partly responsible for the infamous Toubon Law of 1994, which guards the French language against Americanisms, Arabisms, and the word play that makes up the slang of the banlieues (the zones of high-rise project housing, sub-standard schooling and high unemployment that encircle French cities). The NTM affair (and subsequent media attention to Joey Starr's assault of a flight attendant) has helped the group secure platinum sales, a multi-record deal with Epic-Sony and a contract with Adidas. While lamenting money's tendency to "rot people" ("L'argent pourrit les gens"), Joey Starr and Kool Shen have established production companies (IV My People and Boss), which have released albums by new artists like Busstaflex and Zoxea. Both NTM and compatriots IAM provide vivid vibrant counterpoint to the slack moneyed-up triumphalism of their US rapping counterparts.

N.W.A.

Straight Outta Compton

(STRAIGHT OUTTA COMPTON, RUTHLESS/PRIORITY,1989)

"You are now about to witness the strength of street knowledge. . ."

Proof that it's not always about the music. Proof that sometimes the music can be the only redemptive factor. N.W.A. were everything everyone said about them, and a whole lot less. For a few choice minutes like "Express Yourself", "8 Ball", "Fuck Tha Police", "100 Miles And Runnin'" and, especially, the title track of their second album, *Straight Outta Compton*, they were totally irresistible. Nonetheless, it's often forgotten how sparsely great N.W.A. were. The reason they've been elevated to such a lofty status in hip hop history is more to do with the new audience they found for rap, the new visibility they had, rather than any lasting lyrical or musical influence they actually wielded. An oft-stated and bloated cliché needs lancing here: N.W.A. didn't start gangsta rap. It had existed for years, and it had developed well beyond the bracingly primitive version with which N.W.A. gained such airtime. Ultimately, for many, the real shock surrounding N.W.A. was not to be found in their lyrics or videos or biographies. What startled you was that the ultra-conservative arm of the music-censorship movement had finally caught up with the sick shit going on in the underground.

This particular moral panic about music was luckily given an extra, racial kick up the slippery pole of grown-up news agendas worldwide, and so N.W.A. were firmly on the road into young, suburban hearts'n'minds.

But what wonderful hokum coloured that rise; what chaff was spun into gold. In the US, tales of FBI wire-taps, and threatening letters from the same agency. In the UK, the authorities dusted off the Obscene Publications Act and seized copies of *Efil4Zaggin'* the group's final release. Island won them back. Crusty backbenchers bemoaned filth to the cameras in Parliament Square. Though N.W.A.'s serious threat to western democracy in songs as dangerously puerile as "Findum, Fuckum & Flee" and "To Kill A Hooker" was never explicitly made clear by anybody, fuck me was it thrilling to see hip hop blow all those carefully secreted pink tutus up so many pompous arseholes.

The pensive worry of well-meaning liberals was even more gruesome than the right's antique outrage. There were those who wept and wailed that hip hop was getting split down the centre, that there'd be a war for the hip hop audience between the good guys (De La, the JBs, Tribe, Run-DMC, PE) and the baaaad (everyone else), a war that the flashier, more sexy, criminal-minded hip hop would inevitably win. Ignoring the fact that most hip hop fans were quite capable of listening to both without torturous self-analysis, ignoring the fact that, sonically, the last two N.W.A. albums were just about the most desperately faithful PE-tribute albums ever made.

Crucially, once the shock had blown out, the band (a band assembled in a drug-financed office by a failed impresario called Eazy-E, lucky enough to have Dr Dre and Ice Cube walk through his door with songs no one else would record) had disintegrated. Dre was off on his first, global putsch. Cube was becoming a star. The rest were lost. But don't let anyone tell you N.W.A. were a hullabaloo about nothing. For the duration of the astonishing *Straight Outta Compton*, they were the most exhilarating sound west-coast hip hop had given us by 1989, with Dre painfully aware of the limitations of Eazy's finances but still jacking noise together with such windmilling ferocity its effect is primeval. And each verse was an unforgettable pearl from the swine trough. Cube's wickedly timed, "You too boy if ya fuck with me", rhyming "keep you dancin'" with "Charles Manson", that crucial breath between "I'm knockin' niggaz out tha box" and "daily". MC Ren veering from new man ("I'm a call you a bitch or dirty-ass ho") to beatnik ("Look, you might think that it's a trip"). Eazy slurring "Dangerous motherfucker raises hell", the toothy grin you can imagine him flashing in between "And when I see a punk pass. . ." and ". . . I smile".

After the newspapers and scripts have been lost in landfills, moments like these are N.W.A.'s finest, the reason they'll always be held in affection and not mild regret. The perceived and therefore self-perpetuating victory N.W.A.'s brand of rap had won meant that for much of the early- to mid-nineties, those supposedly in the know were looking down the creative cul-de-sac of G-Funk while the rest of rap carried on motoring away in a different direction. They've never really caught up.

With Cube the map-reader gone, NWA tours fell foul of Eazy's substandard navigational skills.

OUTKAST

Hey Ya

(SPEAKERBOXXX/THE LOVE BELOW, LA FACE, 2003)

"Now don't have me break this thang down for nothin'/Now I wanna see y'all on y'all baddest behaviour. . ."

The decision – whether to represent Outkast with "Elevators (Me And You)", their breakthrough hit from '96's *ATLiens*, or this, their most recent hit – did cause me some agony. Ultimately, it's a choice between basking in hip hop's glorious past (which much of this book unapologetically wallows in) and proposing that hip hop has a bold and vibrant future ahead of it. I chose the latter, though I feel Outkast don't share my optimism. What's so wonderful about the miracle that is Outkast is that though they've given so much to hip hop, you always get the feeling that their musical invention and gratifying indulgence is animated by a disgust towards the rest of rap. From *ATLiens* on, each successive Outkast masterpiece has found itself increasingly isolated from the rest of planet rap. So *Speakerboxxx/The Love Below* is a record without precedent, perhaps the first true masterwork of this millennium's hip hop. Yet it never suggests that these are ideas that others should pick up on, work with, co-opt. Rather its glorious uniqueness repels all comparison, resists all attempts to fit it in with any broader trends.

If hip hop may find it impossible to take on what Outkast have done, what hip hop can and always should admire and attempt to attain is Outkast's genuine disinterest in the rest of rap, the way they look inward and forward but never back, never over their shoulder.

It's been thus since their debut, *Southernplayalisticadillacmuzik*, hit the Top 20 in 1994 and was certified platinum by the end of the year. The suite of LPs that followed, '98's *Aquemini* and 2000's *Stankonia*, were perhaps the most bizarre, left-field, yet compulsively chartable hip hop of rap's third decade, lifting Outkast up from the level of being originators (alongside Goodie Mob) of the Dirty South hip hop renaissance to internationally acclaimed, pop innovators. But 2003's frightmarish, fractious *Speakerboxxx/The Love Below* was a twin-album set that managed to bewilder fans and critics alike – so far out it was suggestive of a creative schizophrenia Outkast would never be able to repeat without being sectioned.

While Big Boi's *Speakerboxxx* was a typically all-encompassing Outkast album (and a stunningly executed one at that), Andre 3000's *The Love Below* was more like the great lost Prince album that should've followed *Sign O' The Times* – a sprawling opus that investigates love, death, fatherhood, suicide, sex, drugs, rock'n'roll and Andre's own tortured experience of all the above in songs arranged like some demented revision of the seventies, epic soul he so clearly wanted to recreate.

Within the context of *Speakerboxxx/The Love Below*, "Hey Ya" makes a weird kind of sense. Out on its own as a single, it makes an even more startling kind of sense. This is psychedelia, no question; this sounds like Love, the Electric Prunes, Barrett-era Floyd, some off-cut from a Nuggets compilation, some great, lost, little seven-inch from 1967 that you'll spend your life trying to find anything like. The fact that Andre threw in some elements that dragged it away from that easy space (a devastating Casio riff and some Kraftwerk bleeps, the sheer, existential desperation of Andre's vocal) makes it all the more uniquely Outkast's. No one else on earth would think of making music this throwaway, this unforgettable, this instant and this endless. And while the idea of Outkast could've been weakened by a double album such as this, *Speakerboxxx/The Love Below* proves, on the contrary, that Andre and Big Boi will never find such mutually understanding people to work with in their lives. If their relationship is on its last legs, I pray they get sucked into carrying on 'cos the spite and lunacy are better represented on "Hey Ya" than on anything since Sly Stone in his drugged-up prime. Essential.

The highest state of the art. Outkast

It's Real

(GUERILLA FUNK, PRIORITY, 1999)

"And everybody wanna be a Gee, the same sick house nigga mentality/Please, fuckin' with them fake fairytales. . ."

If Public Enemy put the bit in your teeth, then Paris made you bite down hard. A lot of the education, much self-imparted, that many of us followed up on at the instigation of the first three Public Enemy LPs left us hungry, both mentally and musically. The listening and reading list that PE set us was a start, but we wanted more music that picked up on PE's trailblazing mix of political bite and musical innovation. Paris provided that immediate satisfaction, but he also provided a lot more: reading about oppression and racism necessarily creates bile in your gut, a rage and a frustration at an authority seemingly beyond your grasp. While PE always seemed way ahead of your head – this stunning work of art you'd spend the rest of your life trying to decipher – and somehow more adult in attitude than you were, Paris seemed to be someone who had no problem indulging in sheer spite at the powers-that-be.

There's a gleeful hatred to Paris's opening two albums, *The Devil Made Me Do It* and *Sleeping With The Enemy* (an album Tommy Boy refused to release because of the track "Bush Killa") that ensures they still sit atop some of the truly great, agit-rap acts who'd sprung up in PE's wake. Seek out Consolidated's *The Myth Of Rock*, *Friendly Fascism*, *Play More Music* and *Business Of Punishment* albums, Chill EB's "Born Suspicious" EP, Movement Ex's eponymously titled LP and The Coup's *Kill My Landlord* for more on that story. What made Paris particularly appealing to a generation who'd had their minds revolutionized by PE, but needed an outlet for all the angst PE had engendered in them, was that he sounded like a fan, like us. It helped that both LPs had a Bomb Squad fixation as deep as our own; it sealed the deal when we realized Paris had his own ferocious intelligence and personality that could swing from gut-level rage to high-minded political philosophy in the space of a verse. He was like us. Only way more militant and way, way smarter. This was a guy we were gonna stick with.

By the time Paris had taken Tommy Boy to court, released *Sleeping With The Enemy* on his own Scarface imprint with the settlement money (he had an economics degree and a legal knowledge that helped him way in the future when he went on sabbatical as a successful stockbroker) and emerged with *Guerilla Funk* in 1994, he'd taken on less the mantle of a comrade than that of a wintry, isolated hero. By then, we were in the depths of the G-Funk revolution, a movement in rap that provided as many musical delights as it did lyrical frustrations. What was so blazingly righteous and cool about "It's Real" was that it was a spot-on P-Funk-inspired, musical masterpiece, easily as lush as the narco-funk cruise-control Dre was perfecting at the same time but with its lyrical focus diametrically opposed to gangsta's disempowerment (for all of Snoop's and Warren G's claims of control, they always sounded to PE fans like pawns in the scheme of The Man). Here was George Clinton's musical magic pulled back from its deterioration into soundtracking urban demise, used instead to re-energize minds bludgeoned into depressed submission as gangsta ravaged all before it.

It recalled instantly the positive statements of the original Parliament albums, but put them together in a vicious, timely way that could leave no doubt: not only did Paris have better lyrics than most gangsta-rappers, he could arrange the intricacies of gangsta-funk better than anyone. The hilarious, vehement way "It's Real" both lampooned gangsta for its dishonesty and lack of vision, while offering a living, breathing alternative to that creative dead end was a blessed relief in an era when we were told that the confirmation of negative stereotypes was the only future rap could call its own. Paris came back in 2003 with the typically calm and collected *Sonic Jihad*. Nice to know some firebrands can't shake the spark.

PETE ROCK & C.L. SMOOTH

All The Places

(THE MAIN INGREDIENT, ELEKTRA/ASYLUM, 1994)

"Travelling the warp speed we come to the peak/Like a missile I probe and seek, many can't critique. . ."

Great things about a lot of hip hop LPs are the opportunities for distraction. Most rap albums are too long – fact. It's one of the perils of CDs that many albums in all genres have turned into over-indulgent wankfests that won't fit on one side of a tape, combined with the over-ambitiousness of mediocre talents, that guest-spot cameo given up as a favour for a friend they're seriously thinking about dumping soon, the misplaced dedication track or unfunny skit heralding every B-boy's chance to put the kettle on, or concentrate on the joint they're rolling, or flick their blaupunkt over to *Gardeners' Question Time*. Pete Rock never gave you that opportunity. It'd take you half an hour to roll that spliff, cos the sheer quality of what he was pushing into your life took up all your space, took you out to space without the need for dope-smoke or coke-mirrors.

Even now, there's a warm, narcotic buzz that creeps down your body, from scalp to toe, with particular, massaging effects on your shoulders, whenever you even think about Pete Rock's triple-shot of devastating hip hop that started with *Mecca And The Soul Brother* in '92, continued through *The Main Ingredient* in '94 and wound up with *Soul Survivor* in '98. The first two were touchstone recordings for an unashamed, new trend in hip hop listening: they were albums you heard on headphones with a big-assed J on the go, nodding your head and twitching your roaches 'til the dawn. A sacred tablet for the whole trip-hop axis (that fundamentally spun out the kind of instrumentals

Rock threw down for Smooth to yawn-inducing length), the music on *The Main Ingredient* can be seen as the moment when hip hop started realizing that it could take the lessons it learnt from jazz and funk and dub in a determinedly musical and spiritual direction, focus in on the soul of the music as much as its sonic detail. This wasn't music that used jazz (in the sense that so much bad jazz-hop wore jazz like a fucking armband), it re-invoked it, recovered its musical spirit of precise restraint and total freedom, and applied it to hip hop. Like the boho-hip sleeve notes said: "We are the planters of the weeds or roses in our garden. Take the plunge within yourself and find THE MAIN INGREDIENT." We did. And we got the munchies real bad.

Only his mentor Marley Marl matched PR for consistent, instinctive, studio magic. When *The Main Ingredient* dropped, Rock had Premo and others nipping at his heels, but there's a relaxed, nothing-to-prove and effortlessly great feel to the grooves on this album that seals it in the heart firmer than anything else from 1994. Smooth is the Ringo Starr of rapping: simple, straight-ahead, utterly misunderstood by arseholes who mistake fuss for depth, organically enmeshed in the music as much as the drum patterns, the propulsive lo-end, the weird touch PR would throw into every track that would hook it into your brain forever. The opening, double-sucker-punch of "In The House" and "Carmel City" fades into the seriously addictive undulations and impacts of "I Get Physical" and you know you're home and it's heaven. It's only topped by the incredible "All The Places" – a mix of sixties pop, deep funk and Philly soul so exquisite your skin puckers every time you hear it. In a rap market at the time dominated by the dull rumblings of a Diddy man in the east and Suge Knight in the west, Rock and Smooth were both inspirational and depressingly unrewarded for their greatness. They were always just a little bit more mortally humble and coolly godlike than anyone else. Oh, is anyone going to the all-night garage? Could you pick us up two packets of Monster Munch and a Bounty and a Pepperami and. . .

THE PHARCYDE

Oh Shit

(BIZARRE RIDE II THE PHARCYDE, DELICIOUS VINYL, 1992)

"I got a funny feeling like something was real wrong/Looked at her shoes and her feets was real long. . ."

Of course, they were dancers. A fact often forgotten, but The Pharcyde, one of the most off-the-hook, out-the-park, alterno-rap acts ever, didn't meet up on street corners, at jams or in record stores: they were dancers and choreographers who met on the late-eighties, underground club circuit in LA, worked together for a while and served a stint as dancers on the Fox network's comedy-variety series, *In Living Color*.

MCs and producers Tre "Slimkid" Hardson, Imani Wilcox, and Romye "Booty Brown" Robinson hooked up with Derrick "Fatlip" Stewart in 1990. Under the tutelage of Reggie Andrews, a local high school music teacher, the group learned about the music industry and recording before landing a deal with Delicious Vinyl in 1991 and releasing the stunning *Bizarre Ride...* a year later. They were as fast-moving as their music, and you can hear something of the terpsichorean throughout that debut. Everything's danceable, perfect for moving to. and if you didn't wanna shake your booty then the rhymes themselves would transport you into hidden realms without you even leaving your seat. Oft-forgotten now, *Bizarre Ride...* was one of the great, early-nineties rap LPs for those looking for an alternative to the suffocating insularity of gangsta.

The sleeve was one hell of a tip-off that this wasn't gonna be yer normal hip hop LP – a roller coaster drawn with all the slapdash skill of a Hanna-Barbera background artist. And then, when you flipped the cover over, you suddenly saw that the car The Pharcyde were riding was about to be sucked into the tooth-edged vagina of a colossal, rail-limbed floozy. "Oh Shit", twenty seconds into the album, was the next clue, a hysterically funny three-parter about those moments in life where "Oh shit!" comes to your lips, bouncing on full-fat, piano-led funk that went beyond the more reverent and polite jazz-hop stylings of A Tribe Called Quest and Gang Starr and resurrected the full, lurid colour of a Cab Calloway or Count Basie.

Isolated on a west coast thoroughly immersed in the gangsta era, The Pharcyde showed that Los Angeles could just as easily draw on its psychedelic and showbiz roots as document South Central's grittiest streets – an inspiration for future California psychonauts like Jurassic 5 and People Under The Stairs.

PHAROAH MONCH

Simon Says

(12", RAWKUS RECORDS, 1999)

"You sold platinum round the world, I sold wood in the 'hood/But when I'm in the street, then shit it's all good. . ."

The record that was meant to take the underground into the mainstream ended up achieving something quite different – making us all realize how petty such distinctions were and how much ground there was to be obliterated. It was disappointing after the explosion of interest in Company Flow and Rawkus Records that so many in the underground underestimated their fan base and saw the indie renaissance as a method of retreat. Happy with their backpacker-audience congregation, Rawkus and the rest of the New York underground busied themselves creating a whole, new, lucrative elitism that sought to demonize all overground rap. After Rawkus broke big, the critics would love any record emerging on an obscure label with a cheap, shitty sleeve. Ignoring the fact that quite a lot of underground hip hop was terrible. Ignoring the fact that the whole idea of a hip hop more "intelligent" than hip hop that sold (a hip hop with more authenticity simply because its business backing was more impoverished) ran totally counter to hip hop's history of reaching out to all. Fatally ignoring the fact that by the late nineties, mainstream hip hop was sounding more musically inventive than the underground (under the auspices of Timbaland in particular). Crucially, by 1999, the sham that was the New York underground rested on a fundamental misunderstanding of the hip hop audience, always way more agile as consumers than the demographers and marketeers would have you believe, just as able to dig Jay-Z and Mos Def, Missy and Sarah Jones. "Simon Says" proved that both mainstream and underground audiences responded to one thing: great music. And it destroyed the old dichotomies between underground and mainstream in one fearsome belch of noise.

As a member of NYC duo Organized Konfusion, Monch had already developed a rep as one of underground hip hop's finest wordsmiths, crafting some genuinely mind-blowing raps with partner Prince Poetry: cut loose on Rawkus, Monch's guest appearances on the *Soundbombing* comps and other people's cuts whet the appetite for when he'd drop his solo shit. *Internal Affairs* was a great album, but "Simon Says" leapt out from it like Godzilla. It was dissed by underground snobs who felt Monch was deserting his roots, but when the monstrous horn loop pivotal to "Simon Says" came roaring into your life, it was clear that Monch himself didn't give a fuck about such petty categorizing. He produced the track himself to become the most extreme a mainstream track could ever get, the most instantly appealing an underground track could ever be. The confusion and delightful oddity of a track with such indie roots becoming a club smash in the summer of '99 was the last wonderful irony hip hop gave us in that millennium.

Rawkus' finest wordsmith, Pharoah Monch.

PUBLIC ENEMY

Brothers Gonna Work It Out

(FEAR OF A BLACK PLANET, DEF JAM, 1990)

"3 stones from the sun, we need a piece of this rock/Our goal indestructible soul. . ."

This book could've begun and ended with Public Enemy, with around seventy of their songs in between. In a text that's often about the "relative" importance of certain tracks, certain bands, Public Enemy are difficult to squeeze in anywhere without squeezing everything else out. For a band with such an undeniably immense influence on the history of rap music, what's instantly memorable and most intimately associated with PE in your mind is just how unique, how disconnected from everyone but themselves they were. And further than that, it's not simply a matter of PE influencing the history of hip hop, of all music. It's the fact that for those pounced on and bitten by *Yo! Bum Rush The Show* in 1987, or *It Takes A Nation Of Millions To Hold Us Back* in 1989, their lives would never be the same again.

My life before Public Enemy is a dimly recollected haze of kids' stuff, building dens, pissing about, not feeling quite like you do now. It's like looking back before a bereavement and wondering who in hell that innocent was who was wearing your skin. Before Public Enemy happened to me, my mind was in a different shape than it is now, my living present and past and future all got re-designed and revolutionized by the mental and social upheaval that PE wrought in my life.

My motivations before then were born of whims, boredom and childish curiosity. After Public Enemy, I wanted nothing more than to achieve the same, steely control over mind and body that they so clearly had. For a lot of us who'd experienced racism, the traditional reactions (shame, hurt pride, bitterness) were all we knew, and they were solitary, lonely experiences, wounds that festered without recovery and separated us from the rest of the happy planet. PE showed us that there was a unity within oppression and that if we simply pushed our mental barriers back a little, we'd realize the place in history, our history, that the rest of the world would seek to deny and deflect us from. They showed us that we weren't alone, they showed us that our experiences could be part-explained as simply the latest symptoms of an ancient lie and the worldwide belief in that lie. And further than that, they put a clench in fists that no longer could be content just digging nails into our palms, that readied themselves for combat. And they made being in on these secrets something that we could be proud of, a mental space we could call our own.

For any band fundamentally to change the aspirations and attitudes of an entire generation is some achievement. For that same band to do it while also creating some of the most utterly transcendent, accurate, revolutionary music ever made in history provides such a glut of riches that I can't and won't compare Public Enemy to anybody else. They were untouchable, beyond any shadow of doubt that the slack, retrospective mind might be tempted to consider, the most important band in this book, of this earth, in my life – and so many other lives as well.

PE pulled a coup on your consciousness on two fronts. Run any track from their first two albums next to anything else in rap at the time and you can immediately tell the difference, even before Chuck and Flav start in. As with PE in general, the part that entailed the Bomb Squad's productions has had a huge influence, but still sounds quite unlike anything else in hip hop before or since – it took the innately revolutionary nature of hip hop production (all sound can be fucked with) to its ultimate level of coherency and control. This was nothing short of the creation of a new musical language, built on old dialects and syllables (the same funk loops and beats the rest of hip hop would simply arrange in different orders) but emerging from the sorcery of Keith and Hank Shocklee and Eric Sadler (who, lest we forget, worked similar mind-bending tricks of sound on the Brian Eno-David Byrne album, *My Life In The Bush Of Ghosts*, a decade previously, an album that greatly influenced Chuck D) as a whole new babble whose sense was there to be decoded.

The Bomb Squad created genuinely new sounds, real originality, within an artform that should've been limited to the recycled and familiar. If the rest of hip hop had blown your mind because it suddenly seemed that all bets were off, that all creativity was free and accessible to all and that the old hierarchy of "musicianship" and "craft" was being torn down with a hooligan thirst to make a racket, then PE were the moment when that clear ground really started being investigated, explored, worked on. In all directions. Forward. Back. Up to the skies. Down to hell. Out into space. Into the heart. So much was going on in the sound, yet it all seemed to be there for a reason, each element a vital part of this clockwork, sonic juggernaut that PE rode through your skull. For the first four years of their existence, they were creating music that made everything else sound merely mortal by comparison. And the frightening thing, listening to PE now, is that it's a sound that still hasn't been topped. You don't just recall Public Enemy in purely sonic terms; you recall how the sound looked, how the sound felt, how the sound touched you. PE imparted a sensuality (and that doesn't always have to mean sexuality) and a tactile quality to hip hop production which is rarely acknowledged but which fundamentally shifted the confines of what hip hop music could achieve; where production sat in relation to the MC. For PE, it's still an untouchable triumph. Other producers have attempted it, certainly, but have never achieved the same, divine mix of bedlam and brilliance.

**S1W's, Chuck D, Terminator X
and Professor Griff during
PE's late 80's peak.**

To that bold, new world of sound add the second front of PE's genius, the intellectual and lyrical content coupled with the voices that delivered that message to you, and the greatest band in pop history starts to take definite shape. No one sounds like Chuck D any more, perhaps because so many attempted to and failed, perhaps because there's a perception that D's was an unsubtle voice only suited to the polemics that PE produced. Utterly wrong on all counts. Chuck D was just as good when being conversational ("You're Gonna Get Yours'"), in parody mode ("Pollywannacracka"), freestyling ("Timebomb") and abstract ("Night Of The Living Baseheads") as when he was directly trying to change the world.

Whatever the situation, there was never any arguing with that voice; you could hear the steel mesh undergoing the G-force of each syllable, you could hear the vocal booth rattling in the tornado. Instantly identifiable and yet utterly bereft of gimmick – this is Chuck's voice, the way he speaks, and it was always as capable of contradiction and confusion (recall the desperately pressured rhymes of "Welcome To The Terrordome") as it was of conviction and condemnation. Vital to keeping hold of you as a listener was the relationship of Chuck's voice to Flav's. It wasn't just that Flav was such a freewheeling, laugh-riot nutcase-supreme next to Chuck's more authoritarian personality, it was that Flav's voice (high-pitched and petulant where Chuck's was booming and angry) formed such a glorious counterpoint to D's, it was the stick that unfurls a flag saying "bang" from a toy gun next to Chuck's lyrical bullets.

And the way that PE's message is frequently simplified and characterized as merely a modern spin on old, black-power motifs sells the complexity of Chuck's and Flav's narratives horrendously short. There was always as much abstract beat poetry and personal revelation in Chuck'n'Flav's flows as there was direct sloganeering (and as a band that introduced new phrases to the English language with every track, PE were great at sloganeering), always as much humour and heart as there was cold analysis. PE's effect was total, not specific or easily pinpointed. They made being alive different, they charged the global and the intimate with new perspective.

"Brothers Gonna Work It Out" is the track I finally picked because it showcases everything that made PE great – the irreverent alchemy with which they mixed their sources (an old funk bassline, Prince's guitar from "Let's Go Crazy") to create gold, their vocal power (the way Chuck and Flav bounce off each other is as gleeful as it is immaculate) and the unfathomable depths of what they'd rap about. "Brothers Gonna Work It Out", like the album it kick-starts (*Fear Of A Black Planet* – still their artistic masterpiece), is a track that seethes with infinite questions, blazes on its own fuel of musical invention and lethal lyricism, and still sounds like music and language re-imagined and re-tooled for the battle that we found ourselves fighting in 1990, emerging from the black-and-white certainty of our adolescence into a more complex and doubtful adult future. And like all good PE, it's an endless track, it's a track that still richly rewards listening, a track that seems to suggest so much that's remained unexplored.

And that's perhaps PE's lasting legacy to the world, the fact that they spun so many of us out of the lives pre-programmed for us and taught us the values of self-education, self-extension, transcendence despite and through self-awareness. I can trace every single record I own back to PE because when they crashed into my life, they were the first to suggest that music was not just entertainment to be enjoyed but could offer a whole, alternative way of looking at the universe, a way of connecting the disparate and reflecting the chaos both external and internal that until then had remained inchoate and unresolved.

They got us interested in life, in something more than ourselves. For that hint alone, that led so many of us to so much more, we should declare our love and gratitude every time PE get mentioned anywhere. Before PE, the future loomed unknowable but probably dull. After PE, there was no looking back, and the future was there to be imagined and re-imagined by all of us. If you get only one track mentioned in this book, make it this one. PE lead everywhere else.

REDMAN

Green Island

(DARE IZ A DARKSIDE, RAL, 1995)

"I wrreerawwwowww like Anthrax, split my pants like Bill Bixby. . ."

When Christina Aguilera cashed in her ghetto-pass by getting Redman to guest on "Dirrty" (and in the lamentable, kiddie-porn video), it was quite possibly the most surreal sight that Redman has ever given us. Which is up against some stiff competition.

Reggie Noble's one of those talents in rap who inspires euphemisms such as "maverick" and "one-off" when what people really mean can be expressed in far more direct and less sensitive language. Put plainly, Redman's a fucking hatstand, barking, a headcase. It's the kind of insanity that gets on with life but is undoubtedly touched by drugs. Not fast, self-improving, business-like drugs. Not even sexy, urban drugs. Just provincial, deranging, slow-building, long-lasting, powerful hallucinogens that twist you out of shape for life. Acid, mushrooms, peyote, DMT. When Redman breathed on you with his debut, *Whut? Thee Album*, you got a contact high that lasted for weeks.

Redman's here because he represents all hip hop artists who imprinted themselves on a culture that prizes teamwork with totally individual works of art. Like fellow-loons ODB, Chino XL, New Kingdom, MC 900ft Jesus, Bubba Sparxxx, he has a talent that's his own but it's a talent so freewheelingly unconcerned with where it fits that you can't help but think it's an ability stumbled upon, not nurtured, that we're lucky hip hop spoke to him before the voices coming from his radiator drowned it out. Redman's absolute lack of worry about what people think about him, his ability to look like a drug-ravaged Vietnam vet who thinks New Jersey is Saigon, the apocryphal stories about him doing disgraceful, rent-boy things with people just to score acid, that cracked, ravaged, bewildering and bewildered voice – all of this conspires to turn him into a B-boy's hero even as we admit we're glad we don't have people like him in our lives. . . even though every time you check the mirror

A face you can trust from New Jersey's favourite son, Redman.

the afternoon after the night before, you realize there's a little bit of Reggie Noble in all of us. Lucky fucker's never had to snap out of it.

It's the fact he came from New Jersey that explains Redman's self-medicated strangeness. The Bricks (his home patch and an ultra-squalid area of NJ) is a corner of America where the people have been forgotten about, and where the people can forget about America. If Red's debut set *Whut?* was all about striking out from such a shithole, his follow-up, the astonishing *Dare Iz A Darkside*, was about returning to that concrete birthplace because it's the only place that feels like home, the only place that can actually make sense of your senselessness, the only place where you feel something approaching sanity, the only place you'd wanna be when the flashbacks and the trips come pulling you outside.

"Green Island" is the album's epicentre and mind-melting highlight, a woozy, progressively more engulfing fog of blunted-assed, stop-start beats, shimmering Hawaiian guitar cutting through like a tropical heatwave, the snares making your seat wave, some hysterically funny, drugged-up and drunk doggerel and the most puerile fade-out you ever pissed yourself laughing to. One of the towering, psychedelic moments in hip hop history.

ROB BASE & DJ EZ ROCK
It Takes Two

(7" SINGLE, PROFILE 1988)

"I'm not internationally known
But I'm known to rock the microphone"

Monster pop smash from a soon-disbanded Harlem duo that rapidly became
the most oversampled record in rap: samples from Motown and JB (Lynn
Collins' similarly over-ravaged "Think (About It)" formed the basis of "It Takes
Two") rattle past and it's difficult remembering that this was original at the
time when so much grim exactly-the-same-sample-bank plundering went on
directly afterwards. Base's dumb-as-a-post lyrics still charm but what "It Takes
Two" proved to a lot of us (and I'm speaking as someone who RAN to the shop
to buy it in '88) is something startling for any B-boy to acknowledge. That hip
hop, like other music, has a lifespan, starts to sound stale with overexposure,
starts to be just as annoying as the rest of pop can when you're over
saturated. A wake-up call from a coma of adolescent uncritical acceptance we
all needed to be shaken out of.

Table Of Contents

(THINGS FALL APART, MCA, 1999)

"You talkin' all this shit out your mouth, you satanic/Roam the planet, always takin' bullshit for granted. . ."

If one thing is anathema to hip hop it's hippiedom, especially the kind of live-instrumentation, boho bollocks that gets old-fart rock fans nodding their heads and waving rap acts through the gate just because they know which end of a guitar to play. Hip hop doesn't need such validation from all those "keep-music-live" cretins: if you'd only known about The Roots from their press over the past five years, you might have avoided them, believing them to be the patchouli-ponging rash of their unfortunate and unfair portrayals.

Truth is, yeah, The Roots use live instruments, though not for reasons of muso credibility. Back in 1987, when rapper Black Thought (Tariq Trotter) and drummer ?uestlove (Ahmir Khalib Thompson) became friends at the Philadelphia High School for Creative Performing Arts, the duo had no money for the DJ essentials – two turntables and a microphone, plus a mixer and plenty of vinyl. So they recreated classic hip hop tracks with ?uestlove's drum kit backing Black Thought's rhymes. Playing around school, on the sidewalk and, later, at talent shows, the pair began to earn money and hooked up with bassist Hub (Leon Hubbard) and rapper Malik B (Malik Abdul Basit).

The Roots' first major-label album, *Do You Want More?!!!??!*, was released in January 1995. Forsaking usual, hip hop protocol, the album was produced without any samples or previously recorded material. Taking their now blazing live show (and no one tops The Roots live) on Lollapalooza, The Roots smartly hired human beatbox Rahzel, the "Godfather of Noyze" – previously a performer with Grandmaster Flash and LL Cool J – and Scott Storch (later Kamal). 1996's *Illadelph Halflife* was the real leap-off point, a startlingly honest look at keeping a band together through industry ignorance and touring madness, shot through music that sampled their live performances but was as spectral and affecting as Outkast.

By the time '99's *Things Fall Apart* came out, The Roots had located a bold, new space in hip hop. Using live instruments but creating a sound way more abstract and studio-spun than you'd expect, it was the way The Roots bent their own playing so wickedly out of shape, used only what was vital, that was so astonishing. While the realer-than-thou, indie-rap underground had merely inverted the mainstream's playa braggadocio (we expected a grimy, New York 12" called "Proud To Be Poor" any minute), The Roots always dealt in a more doubtful, politicized engagement with the problems of maintaining artistry in hip hop. The stunning, Sun Ra-esque jazz chaos of "Table of Contents" was a precise detonation of both mercenary and realist impulses in rap, while the incredible, textual riot in which The Roots surround their musings was never less than utterly absorbing. They created, perhaps, rap's first melancholy masterpiece. On "Table Of Contents", there's a downered, fragmented feel to the music that weaves through the lyrics' bleak resignation to instill real poignancy and effect. The Roots remain a fearsomely intelligent yet forlorn inspiration for anyone daring to step to a mic or a deck as rap stumbles into the future.

RUN-DMC

Sucker MCs

(RUN-DMC, PROFILE, 1984)

"You five dollar boy and I'm a million dollar man/Youse a sucker MC, and you're my fan. . ."

Let's get this straight. There's always been a tendency in rap to pay homage to the early hip hop heroes en masse, giving it up for pretty much everyone who came to the mic in the eighties just because if rappers don't stick up for old rappers, who will? And also because if hip hop history isn't remembered, it can't be subverted and taken in different directions, and the culture loses its shape, its identity. But if we can't deal critically with that past, then talking about it loses its meaning in a welter of undifferentiated affection. Some early rap sounds unmitigatedly shit now, simply because as with any culture so huge in development, some of the antecedents of where we are now are bound to sound cloddish. Not bracingly primitive. Cloddish. Such an elementary fact of cultural growth should be readily acceptable, but where there's elitism and nostalgia, there will be those who see hip hop's chronological progress as its cultural reverse, who think a return to the good, old-skool days is what's needed to get hip hop back (i.e. to make sure hardly anyone's into it anymore). That spoddish, I-was-there-first mentality infects an attitude that says Thou Shalt Not Diss The Heroes! And Run-DMC are definitely among those heroes.

Weird for a crew with the slightly effeminate, original name of Orange Crush. That mixed rock guitars into their beats. That went so often outside of

hip hop for a new audience, new collaborators (unforgettably with Rick Rubin and Aerosmith for "Walk This Way"), new sparks in their two-decade long career. All of which I totally admire, all of which puts them in my list of greats, because they were a huge part of hip hop's acceptance into the mainstream. This would ordinarily estrange them from that particular, hip hop, vinyl-snob, record-collector mindset – but somehow, those people forgive them. Weirder still, the fact that for more than half of Run-DMC's career they were musically lost and pointless seems not even to be mentioned any more. Maybe because the great records they did make, like "Sucker MCs", are so good they make you want to forget the lean years, the lucrative remixes, the born-again Christian years, the duets with Joan Rivers, the fall-off. And remember that for a good chunk of the eighties, Run-DMC were so fucking cool it hurt.

Black Wranglers, black leather, black sweats, black hats – it was easy to copy and it hid so much. In an era when rappers could legitimately wear shoulder pads and shed enough sequins to last Sisqo a lifetime, Run-DMC's stripped-down look and sound seemed the perfect antidote to the danger hip hop was running of getting sucked into being a mere detail of R&B. They were a redefinition of the boundaries, a sure statement of affirmation for a culture which had had its birth-yelp but now needed to say what it damn well wanted. Though hits with metal bands and a pointless remix were DMC's biggest chart moments, it's the original B-side of the original version of "It's Like That" that

remains their defining moment. "Sucker MCs" held the next half-decade of NYC, hardcore hip hop inside its icy grip. Indeed, though battle rhymes and MC-dissing were already well-practised artforms, after "Sucker MCs" no rap act could say it had truly arrived if it didn't have at least one track that called every other rapper on earth a no-talent motherfucker.

Although DMC were never that vulgar, and the rhymes on "Sucker MCs" seem timid in comparison to similar statements of omnipotence we've heard since, the track is genuinely intimidating thanks to the sheer, brutal, mechanoid power of the drum-machine beat and the ferocity of Jam Master Jay's scratching. It's a track that many have signposted as the birthplace of modern rap. When somebody figures out what "modern rap" means, that might be relevant. But what still counts is that Run-DMC were, for all their street credibility, perhaps the most professionally minded of old-skool's heroes and in the seriousness and dedication they brought to hip hop, they were models of a self-sufficient strength that should still be recognized and emulated today. The first rap group shown on MTV, the first to appear on the cover of *Rolling Stone*, the first to have a gold album, the first to hold on to this thing called hip hop and say, "We can do this, it's ours." Original, invincible.

The original Kings Of Rock in their heyday.

Saturday Night

(12", SCHOOLLY D RECORDS, 1986)

"Some call it Cheeba, some call it weed/It's the killer, it's the filler, it's the thing that you need. . ."

The pioneer of gangster hip hop never called himself that, never even admitted that what he created in the mid-eighties should be called "gangsta" at all, even though tracks like "P.S.K. What Does It Mean?" and "Saturday Night" were ripped and sampled by a whole generation of wannabe gangsters for much of the ensuing decade.

What separates rappers like Schoolly and Kool G from the gangsta rappers of the nineties who took on their bleak realism is that they never sounded like they were main players, they never sounded dumb enough to suggest they were actually career criminals. They always sounded more like war reporters, nosey bastards, using what they saw around them every day as the background to set their own characters in motion. Once a member of Philly's notorious Parkside Killers gang, Schoolly burst into hip hop in 1986 with his

self-released, eponymously titled album. It was a record that not only redefined the accuracy with which hip hop would document the streets it soundtracked but was also smart enough to throw in things hip hop had never done before (although it would do from then on) – things like listing clothes brands, the goods Schoolly aspired to owning, all with a new, harshly hardened attitude that defined a new breed of Reaganite hoodlum, thirsty for wealth on a demented quest for the totems of success.

Schoolly unashamedly talked about crack-dealing, about defending your turf, about the scum that collects in the lowest folds of the underbelly. The brutal yet cinematic arrangement of "Saturday Night" was the prototype for hardcore gangsta rap: pared-down beats, showcasing the scarifying testimony of an MC who never seemed to be addressing you from a stage or a vocal booth, always actually seemed to have you by the lapels and pressed against a wall while he demanded a fucking good reason why he should let you stay alive. Still sounding ill like he forever will.

SHOWBIZ & A.G.

Neighbahood Sickness

(GOODFELLAS, PAYDAY, 1995)

"I'm strange, deranged, mentally disturbed/A lunatic that's soon to flip on any nigga (Word). . ."

Out near the Patterson projects and the Bronx Park in the south Bronx is the Bethlehem of rap. Grand Wizard Theodore, Flash, Cold Crush Brothers and Boogie Down Productions all used to jam here. And it's this fertile, holy ground in rap history that gave us Showbiz & A.G.

Show started DJing after witnessing Flash perform in the middle of the Bronx Park basketball courts. He hooked up with Andre The Giant when they were both working on Lord Finesse's debut album, *Funky Technician*, in Jazzy Jay's north Bronx studio (where Finesse, Diamond D, Grand Puba and Brand Nubian all recorded).

Dedicating themselves to "showing that the Bronx is where it started", they released the hugely successful, self-produced, self-pressed "Soul Clap/Party Groove" EP, gaining themselves a deal with Payday in the process and releasing the *Runaway Slave* LP shortly after. Both gave them underground hero status, but by the time their follow-up LP, *Goodfellas*, came out, it was clear that some kind of unholy darkness had seeped into Show & A.G.'s world in the intervening three years.

Goodfellas was perhaps the most evil-sounding masterpiece of mid-nineties, classic, NYC hardcore. Show produced a stunning suite of doomily engrossing sound-clashes, mixing deep, deep dub with the harsh yet blunted beats being cooked up elsewhere by Pete Rock and Premo. On the mic, Diamond D and Method Man helped create a totally locked-on feel of impending disaster: you got the sensation that Show & A.G. weren't much fun to be with at the time, that people were giving them a wide berth because they were clearly off on a mad pursuit of the darkest corners of their imaginations in a place that could only let a little light in, could only be navigated by the two, main protagonists at the album's helm. "Neighbahood Sickness" combines that musical murkiness with a lyrical anger that frequently slips from coherency into pure rage, A.G. unable to find the poison bitter enough to coat his venom-tongued, verbal darts and simply groaning in furiously auto-parasitic loathing. A glorious nadir, a zenith of depression for rap that simultaneously predicted and surpassed the whole, late nineties indie-rap renaissance.

SLICK RICK

The Moment I Feared

(THE GREAT ADVENTURES OF SLICK RICK, DEF JAM, 1988)

"This was the rise and fall of my fast lane style/And I was the main event on the TV for a while. . ."

The "wordsmith from Wimbledon"'s debut LP, *The Great Adventures...* sold 1.2 million copies. Quite apart from the immediate stardom it conferred upon the multi-talented Richard Walters, it's quite staggering to think that over a million households worldwide were inviting someone as charming, funny, poetic yet clearly so caddish into their living rooms.

Blinded by broken glass as an infant, Rick and his eye patch moved with his American-born parents from London back to NYC when he was eleven. In the Bronx, he attended the La Guardia High School of Music and Art, where he became friends with future rapper Dana Dane. The two formed the Kangol Crew, and began performing in hip hop battles around the city. At one 1984 battle in the Bronx, Rick met Doug E. Fresh and began playing with his Get Fresh Crew (which also included Chill Will and Barry Bee). Fresh's Number Four R&B hit, "The Show", exploded just one year later, and MC Ricky D, as Rick was then known, went on to sign a solo deal with Def Jam Records, through his acquaintance with Russell Simmons. For the duration of his debut LP, he is a true poet of profanity – the B-boy Buddha, the greatest living American poet bar none, the original maverick genius of rap. The fact that he was convicted of attempted murder in 1991 and sent upstate (after quickly releasing '91's *The Ruler's Back*) was to ensure Rick's naughty-but-nice, heroic status in the hip hop hall of fame.

The Great Adventures... was a bible with centrefolds, a crude, profane yet deeply mystical trip through the highs and lows of US culture that drew comparisons with French playwright and novelist Jean Genet, American actor and writer Richard Pryor and beat poet and writer Charles Bukowski. Slipping from Diana Ross to Ralph Ellison to whatever the hell flitted through his ravenous intellect, Rick was rap's first truly great storyteller, always willing to slip the leashed confines of his own persona and take on the voices of all the characters in his stories of low-income, enclave life (little girls, big mommas, cops, hustlers, drunks, B-boys). And he performed such vocal tricks with a style, wit, invention and swaggering panache unmatched by anyone.

"The Moment I Feared" is his shining moment because it foregrounds perhaps his greatest legacy to rap: his insistence that you didn't have to sound hard constantly to get heard, his realization that his weird little accent and the soft, almost conversational way he delivered his stories to you were way more effective than the hectoring sermonizing so many others were repetitively locked into. In Rick's brilliantly unmannered vocals, you can hear the roots of Snoop, Eminem and every MC who's come to the mic knowing that they're not in a park battling against other MCs but engaged in an intimate experience with the listener that can be way more complex than freestyling normally allows. And on tracks such as "Treat Her Like A Prostitute" he invented pimpster stylings in hip hop. But the less said about that the better…

SMOOTHE DA HUSTLER

Broken Language

(12", PROFILE, 1995)

"Camera, beer guzzeler, the slug to your mug tuzzeler/The drug juggeler, the crazy thug hustler. . ."

God bless the one-hit wonders, the one-good-album masters. God bless Group Home, Tim Dog, Souls Of Mischief, Nine, Camp Lo, Warren G and, to bring the phenomenon up to date, God bless Clipse, Chingy, Obie Trice and all the rappers who seem to come in blessed with a single, serpentine moment of genius and then have the good grace to disappear from the radar before we can get bored with them. First and foremost, for our purposes here, God bless Smoothe Da Hustler, responsible for one of the all-time, classic, NY tracks, "Broken Language" – still, possibly, the greatest one-off, hip hop hit in history.

Like a lot of rappers who blew into our lives, then just as soon blew out again, Smoothe was first heard on underground mix tapes, tapes that were circulating in New York in 1995. The Brooklynite MC followed up the buzz he was creating with "Broken Language", one of the most staggering linguistic feats pulled off in hip hop history, a track entirely constructed from syntax torn apart and reconfigured as titles Smoothe claims for himself: "The face splitter, gun-totin' hearse initiator, the human drug generator, the Virgin Mary fucker, the Jesus hanger, the idol flipper, the cross breaker and Bible ripper."

It was a track that kicked off on the most banging, phat-assed funk you'd ever heard but as Smoothe opened his mouth and started rapping, you realized that this was something entirely new, that your neck was bristling in the most startling way you'd felt since Rakim or Special Ed. In fact, the track went beyond Rakim, became too much for the mind to handle, refused to stop until Hustler could say anything he liked. And by then, you were locked in and helpless as he squeezed the breath from you in long gasps. It was as if the whole of MCing history was merely a prelude to "Broken Language". Truth be told, Smoothe had more amazing tracks in him ("My Brother My Ace" from the patchy LP *Once Upon A Time In America* retains possibly the most astonishing, line-swapping verse in hip hop history), but "Broken Language" remains the most emblematic and unforgettable one-off rap hit in living memory.

SNOOP DOGGY DOGG

Ain't No Fun (If The Homies Can't Have None)

(DOGGYSTYLE, DEATH ROW, 1993)

"Guess who back in the motherfuckin' house/With a fat dick for your motherfuckin' mouth. . ."

So much of what we heard about Snoop before we actually heard him f'real was designed to throw us off the scent of his real, unique talent. Of course, his contributions to Dre's "Deep Cover" and "Nuthin' But A G Thang" had been noted, but the rest of his story seemed to hint at a real threat, a real nastiness to Snoop that his gentle, loveable persona doesn't really reflect. It was the advance orders that made Doggystyle such a hit, orders doubtless procured in the time between Calvin Broadus getting out of jail (he was three years in and out on drugs charges after leaving high school) and the moment after the 1993 MTV Awards when he surrendered himself to police custody to face murder

charges over an alleged drive-by shooting (he was later cleared). The lurid, criminal detail of Snoop's life boosted interest in him until it seemed the whole world knew his name, knew he'd given a tape to pal Warren G who'd given it to his stepbrother Dr Dre who'd then used Snoop on *The Chronic* to great effect, knew everything about Snoop it was possible to know even if no one had heard his music yet. *Doggystyle*, luckily, lived up to the hype by being a carbon copy of *The Chronic* (never a bad move) and "Ain't No Fun" was the highlight, a gratuitously, gloriously offensive masterpiece of barely controlled menace that showcases one of Dre's most eargasmically sumptuous arrangements under one of Snoop's most distasteful rhymes (worthy of Too Short himself).

What was crucial to Snoop's success (and was a trick none of the gangsta rappers in his wake were interesting enough to develop) was his truly unique character: this wasn't a man who came across instantly as the most

intimidating person you'd ever seen. Rather, he was slight, lanky, gangling, fey. His speech and rapping voice were so mellow they seemed to emerge not from the wide-eyed ferocity of a hoodlum but the red-eyed daze of a perma-stoned rude boy. It was the background of good-time slackerdom that made Snoop's flows so compulsive, the self-awareness he conveyed to you – that even when at his most aggressively criminal, he knew he was fundamentally talking a good game, shooting the breeze about what he knew. *Doggystyle* wasn't an album desperate to please you. Rather, you came to it and sunk into its pace, listened in on Dogg's laconically drawled thoughts.

So when Snoop toured the UK in '94 and Tory politicians wanted him out of the country (mirroring the *Daily Star*'s brilliant "Kick This Evil Bastard Out!" headline), what was shocking was that someone so softly-spoken and polite could arouse such passionate fear. Snoop wisely took a step into the wings after *Doggystyle* and re-emerged later when people had finally realized what a nice young man he really was. "Aint No Fun" sealed this charmer in our lives forever with a fondness that remains undimmed. Along with Dre, perhaps the only worthwhile survivor of the G-Funk years.

'187 on an undercover cop'
Snoop goes deep cover.

SUGAR HILL GANG

Rapper's Delight

(12" SUGAR HILL RECORDS, 1979)

"The rock it to the bang bang boogie say up jumped the boogie/To the rhythm of the boogie, the beat. . ."

Like so many epochal moments in hip hop's genesis, an accident captured on wax. Sugar Hill Gang were recruited on an ad hoc basis by label-founders Sylvia and Joe Robinson – they were to be a novelty act. Big Bank Hank was a former bouncer and pizza waiter who supplied fresh rhymes courtesy of his friend Grandmaster Caz (of Cold Crush Brothers fame). Master Gee, Wonder Mike and Positive Force were all hired on a wing and a prayer to cut a tune Joe Robinson was at first bewildered by. He recalls Sylvia bringing him a fifteen-minute track on a 12" disc. Fifteen-minute tunes didn't get played on the radio but once Joe had secured it only one spin, all hell broke loose. It proved to be the first hip hop single really to sell (eventually shifting eight million copies worldwide, the breakthrough record for old-skool rap and one that informed the industry there was money to be made from this new "fad"). Without it, Sugar Hill wouldn't have been able to give us Funky Four Plus One's "That's The Joint or "The Message" or "White Lines (Don't Do It)". And where we'd all be today, Christ only knows. Listening to it now, it sounds like a relic but what's still startling is how much the bassline actually seems more connected with "Rapper's Delight" than Chic's "Good Times" (the song from which it's filched wholesale). Perhaps the first example of hip hop stealing not just a sample but virtual authorship from the artists it utilized – and still a hip hop party essential to this day.

The Gang's comeback as tag-team wrestlers falters, Wonder Mike unable to fit through the ropes.

Brooklyn-Queens

(THE CACTUS ALBUM, DEF JAM, 1989)

"Do you doubt the shade of vanilla?/I'll play Elvis and you play Priscilla. . ."

White rappers: discuss. OK, there is nothing to discuss. Discussion over.

Seems obvious now that it really doesn't matter about the melanin content of rappers' skin but, back in 1989, 3rd Bass divided hip hop audiences. They were the first white rap act who actually wanted to be taken seriously (the Beastie Boys were always too busy being lunatics to demonstrate any real care about the racial intricacies of their position) by the overwhelmingly black hip hop audience. Enraged by the Beasties' seeming carelessness about the dangers of perceived, cultural imperialism, 3rd Bass were at pains (and sometimes painfully so) to prove their right to be immersed in hip hop culture despite hostility from the press, some fans and other crews. Once the novelty of two spoddy-looking, Jewish, white guys coming out with hip hop wore off, we quickly realized that in *The Cactus Album*, 3rd Bass had created one of the greatest hip hop LPs of the late eighties, an endlessly rewarding, polyglot stew of weird samples (MC Serch and Prime Minister Pete Nice were willing and happy to mix The Smiths with Looney-Tunes sound-fx just to see what happened), inspired linguistic invention and real, lyrical incisiveness thrown together with the help of Prince Paul, Dante Ross and Sam Sever (who had put the initially solo Serch and Nice together).

"Brooklyn-Queens" came at the end of a stunning, hour-long suite of creativity they'd never eclipse again. By the time its final, Fred Quimbyish "pertwang" was echoing around your dome, you knew you could never dismiss a rap act simply for being white ever again. Further than that, you realized that hip hop could only gain from fresh perspectives gleaned from some remove from the hip hop common ground (even though 3rd Bass were both Brooklyn/Queens born'n'bred). 3rd Bass were among the first MCs to suggest that hip hop wasn't about being from a certain race or side of the tracks but about an attitude to music and message, about how the revolutionary techniques of rap could be used to illuminate any lives, any truths of anyone who decided to use them.

A year later, Vanilla Ice was a star but 3rd Bass had already kicked open doors without mindless populism, without compromise to hip hop or themselves. An everlasting inspiration.

The New Rap Language

(B-SIDE OF SPOONIE GEE'S "LOVE RAP", ENJOY, 1980)

"Pump that bass/Do it. . ."

Treacherous Three were one of the most creative of the old-skool pioneers, their super-fast speed-raps creating a whole new style of rapping, one fostered and developed in the white heat of invention that surrounded the burgeoning, hip hop club scene. Totally divorced from all the things that are currently there to help hip hop acts, they symbolize the early struggles of rap back when it had no radio support (until Mr Magic started rocking the pirates), only a handful of clubs it could call home (Disco Fever, T Connection, the Audobon Ballroom and PAL on 122nd street), and its fans were the most isolated in music.

T3 were one of the first groups to make it on to vinyl, and they recorded for both of the major, old-skool labels (Enjoy and Sugar Hill). Formed by a trio of Harlem high-school friends – Kool Moe Dee, LA Sunshine, DJ Easy Lee – and Bronx MC Special K, performing where they could in 1978, they discovered that another high-school friend, Spoonie Gee, who'd just recorded his debut single, was about to drop more wax on Bobby Robinson's Enjoy label (home of Fearless Four and Masterdon Committee). After practising for months, they finally came up with "The New Rap Language", which provided a B-side for Spoonie Gee's 1980 single, "Love Rap".

"The New Rap Language" upped the ante for all other active rappers (and sparked a pair of Treacherous Three/Enjoy classics: "The Body Rock" and "At the Party"). No one before T3 had rapped quite so fluidly, had so summated the state of the art in 1980 but also predicted what would follow in its wake so thoroughly. Perhaps even more than Run-DMC, Treacherous Three were the rhyming model that set a new standard for rap. "The New Rap Language" remains one of the most sampled records in hip hop.

TREACHEROUS THREE

A TRIBE CALLED QUEST

Excursions

(THE LOW END THEORY, JIVE, 1991)

"You could find the Abstract listening to hip hop/My pops used to say, it reminded him of be-bop. . ."

Always best in pop to be looking the other way from where the heat is on, or at least have one eye cocked firmly on the peripheries. Always advisable to dig what the fans, rather than those who imagine they understand those fans, are saying. In 1989, De La Soul's year of dominance, you couldn't get away from the Daisy Age, from De La, from every asshole with a voice in the Press telling you that De La Soul were the most important hip hop group in the world. Possibly true at the time. Probably true in retrospect. But only a fraction of the real story of what was going down in east-coast hip hop at the time, only a hint at the treasures being cooked up elsewhere.

3 Feet High And Rising was the album in most critics' end-of-year lists, but *People's Instinctive Travels And The Paths Of Rhythm*, the debut from NYC four-piece A Tribe Called Quest, was the record that was in most B-boys' racks, upfront, well-thumbed, already scratched to buggery through sheer, addictive overplay. Even now, a decade on, Tribe, especially early Tribe, produce a real emotional pull on rap fans because for so many who grew up with hip hop, ATCQ weren't just a great band – they mark the exact moment that many of us grew up, the moment rap stopped being kids stuff and started making us men.

What Tribe gave us was a definitive and unique reappraisal of what hip hop could talk about, what it could draw from, and what it could and should represent. Before ATCQ, rap was about ego. If it got close up to you, it was always as a prelude to a threat that pushed you back. Rappers ultimately wanted to seduce you and then shut you out, or pull you into their mindset so thoroughly you'd have to relax your own sense of self and subsume it to theirs. Tribe were different.

Over the course of three years and as many albums, you got intimate with their personalities, their music and their words as you would with a friend – with all the doubts and hesitations that would imply. The relationship you developed with DJ Ali Shaheed Muhammed, MC Phife and, especially, leader Q-Tip was conversational, deep, richly rewarding and ever-changing.

Tribe didn't just let you into their lives; they introduced you to the weird rhythms of it, the moments of calm and fury, the abstractions of their minds and the imperatives of their souls. Their music leapt from psychedelia to grit to jazz to pop, as and when the minds behind it demanded. It was as if, after being spoken to by surefire teenagers (which is, after all, what you were at the time) for the entirety of hip hop's late eighties hardcore explosion, here you were suddenly being spoken to as a doubtful adult (which is what, without you noticing, you'd become) by equally open-ended and doubtful adults. Sometimes clueless. Sometimes bohemian and intellectual, sometimes mindless hooligans. But always honest. And for many of us, what we'd expect from hip hop would never be the same again.

Tribe were all born in 1970, a decade on from Bambaataa and with a more confused and chaotic aesthetic sensibility as a result. Their work would employ pop motifs and low-culture references that the more serious elder statesmen of hip hop would consider ephemera, not worthy of rap's light of truth. Forming at school in Manhattan, they started out as founding members of the Native Tongues collective, with contemporaries Latifah and the Jungle Brothers (whose Afrika Baby Bam gave Quest their name). "Description Of A Fool" was their debut in August 1989 and, a year later, "Bonita Applebum" and the *People's Instinctive Travels* album firmly established ATCQ as underground favourites. ("Can I Kick It?" would become an ad jingle as all-pervasively depressing as James Brown's "I Feel Good".)

With a sound that was confected from even more bizarre sources than Prince Paul's creations for De La, and a message way more Afrocentrically minded than those of their Native Tongues allies, Tribe were always the weirdbeards of the stable: their unique perspective and the self-deprecating undercurrent to their rhymes always seemed to be at the point of sabotaging each flow's inherent validity. Thus, Tribe were not just one of the strangest hip hop crews in existence but also responsible for some of the most mind-blowing pop music of the decade. "Excursions" is from their masterpiece, *The Low End Theory*, a deeply dubbed-out, jazz-spooked album that recruited Ron Carter (ex-bassist for Miles Davis and John Coltrane) for extra tones of arse-quaking smokiness.

After the collage-style riot of *Instinctive Travels*, this is Quest finding their true voice, paring down the loops to a brutal minimalism (handy in the years when sample-clearance was becoming a goldmine for greedy old muso dinosaurs) and rhyming deep and demented into the mind's labyrinthine caverns. Concise yet expansive, focused yet bearing the same relation to rap's usual, steely-minded resolve as abstract expressionism does to penny-dreadful, chalk pictures on the pavement. To infinity and beyond.

Ease Back

(CRITICAL BEATDOWN, NEXT PLATEAU, 1988)

"Motivated, as I relate it verbal/Dissing a mouse and smacking any gerbil..."

Kool Keith's first transmission and a hint at the freaked-out, furthest reaches of musical and mental space he was gonna spend his career charting. His first band, Ultramagnetic MC's, were leading lights and avatars of the late-eighties nu-skool, who had their roots in the very first stirrings of rap. Old-skool B-boys who'd emerged from posses such as The People's Choice Crew and New York City Breakers, the Ultramags found each other in the underground's basement clubs, among them Sparkle and the Back Door. DJ Moe Love, TR Love, Ced Gee and ex-psychiatric patient Kool Keith had ideas no one else had: they were the first crew to use a sampler as an instrument, the first to feature extensive use of live instrumentation, the first crew to push rap's sonic sorcery to the limit with a series of mind-blowing singles that had a colossal influence within hip hop and beyond. When the Ultramags used obvious loops, they'd jack the track's speed up, warp and deform the loops until they were unrecognizable. That irreverence toward their sources was a crucial break with the more respectful history of hip hop production. Keith's and Ced Gee's rhymes were delivered in a clipped yet supafast manner that recalled the innovations of Big Daddy Kane and Kool Moe Dee. Where those rappers had been engaged in fairly predictable though enjoyable braggadocio, Kool Keith took hip hop lyrics through strange places, weird arcane references, astral planes, shifting personalities, his uniquely unhinged flow a huge, future influence on everyone from mainstream psychos Xzibit to underground gods Company Flow. Singles such as "Space Groove" and "Ease Back" were club staples that landed the group a deal on the disco-dominated Next Plateau.

The debut LP, *Critical Beatdown*, was under-appreciated at the time but hugely influential retrospectively, not just making an impact on the increased lyrical and musical fearlessness of nineties rap but also being rifled wholesale by artists as diverse as Dr Dre, who sampled the beat from "Funky" for 2Pac's "California Love", and Public Enemy, who used the beat from "Ease Back" for "Terminator X To The Edge Of Panic". UK dance pioneers the Prodigy (whose Liam Howlett was obsessed with the Ultramags) sampled "Give The Drummer Some" on their controversial "Smack My Bitch Up". Kool Keith would go on to create other great records under a myriad of pseudonyms but *Critical Beatdown* and "Ease Back" are still his finest founding statements. Hip hop would never be the same again.

ULTRAMAGNETIC MC'S

WU-TANG CLAN

Protect Ya Neck

(ENTER THE WU-TANG: 36 CHAMBERS, LOUD, 1993)

"First of all, who's your A&R?/A mountain climber who plays an electric guitar. . ."

Try and recall another genre of music that's put moments into your life as revelatory as the first time you heard Public Enemy, Timbaland and, especially, Wu-Tang Clan.

For all the historic lineage of hip hop, the way development can be charted across its narrative, what remain definitive of hip hop history are those moments of alien invasion, total overhaul, complete revolution. Moments linked to what comes before them but only in that they do something none of those previous moments did. Moments that seem to hint at a possible future but are just too uniquely sourced and motivated to be repeated. Any B-boy or B-girl who looks back over their own experience of hip hop knows the records that were suggested by other records, knows the official expansion from New York outwards and all the trails that story took.

But they also know that thrown in the mix are the odd records that seem to have come in from nowhere, beamed in from Venus, in from so far beyond the left field they seem to have been created by a different species of human, one possessed with a language like our own but fascinatingly abstracted from it, a creativity that plays with music in a lunatic, childlike fashion, creating whole new shapes, new words, new lexicons of reference. If being into hip hop often feels like walking sure ground with steady-footed progress, every hip hop fan has to admit that, along the way, there have been moments where the ground has lifted up from under your feet, where you've found yourself at a turning

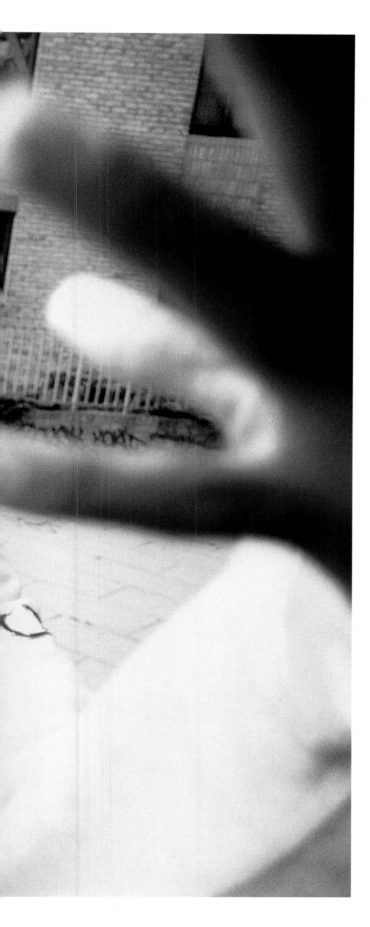

point with countless paths enticing you into dimensions you hadn't even considered before.

Such was your feeling when "Protect Ya Neck" crashed into your life in 1993. Where the fuck did this new way of walking and talking come from? Who the hell were these be-robed, funky monks who seemed to have an obsession with the kung-fu, chop sockey, grindhouse movies of Run Run Shaw? What weird corner of the universe did these psychos call home?

Staten Island, as it happened – perhaps the most neglected of the five boro's, an isolation that had clearly enforced a tangential development in rap with the Wu while everyone was looking somewhere else. Nothing sounded like Wu-Tang in '93. There was something deliciously freakish about the way they rapped and the way they made music. The little we could deduce was tantalizing enough: GZA and Ol' Dirty Bastard (the two founding members), Raekwon, Method Man, Inspectah Deck (aka Rebel INS), U-God, Ghostface Killah, RZA and Masta Killa made up the collective of nine MCs, but even as *Enter The Wu Tang...* broke, you knew that it was merely the testing ground for what was nothing short of an attempted coup on hip hop, which at the time was lost in the heat of the gangsta revolution.

Main ideas man RZA and the rest of the Clan insisted that on signing to BMG as a group, they would each be allowed, contractually, to work as solo artists. Every member, as some (including RZA and GZA) had already done, would go on to release solo records with varying degrees of success, the best still being GZA's *Liquid Swords* and Raekwon's *Only Built 4 Cuban Linx*. But *Enter The Wu-Tang...* was still the release that defined the Staten posse's collective sound and vision.

You could never suspect that this was merely a launch pad for a raft of solo careers because the derangement of syntax and sound is so evenly spread between the Clan members. They were all off on one. The beats and loops the RZA created for his tribe were so bizarre they frequently failed to resemble music. A deeply atmospheric, spine-chilling mix of rugged, primitive funk and ghostly, distorted samples, eerie piano loops, nightmarish echo-plexed dub, it found its apotheosis on "Protect Ya Neck". Within a year of its release, Wu-Tang Clan were the hottest group in rap, making perhaps the strangest music ever to gain mainstream acceptance.

"Protect Ya Neck" was a cataclysmic event for hip hop, infecting rap with a dread ambience that seeped into all of the underground, New York rap that came afterward. It put the driven futurism back into rap at a time when it was in danger of falling into the G-Funk morass. Crucially, it was one of those hip hop tracks that seemed constructed like a Tardis, a hall of mirrors, a labyrinth leading off in a million directions. Like all the best hip hop, not just a definitive, here'n'now moment but also a signpost to a future of infinite possibility. That's why we're into hip hop. That's why we're here.

M.E.T.H.O.D Man welcomes you to Staten Island.

NDEX